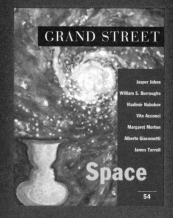

Hilton Als
John Ashbery
Paul Auster
Samuel Beckett

GRAND STREET

William S. Burroughs
John Cage
Alexander Cockburn
William Eggleston
Dennis Hopper
Jasper Johns
Jamaica Kincaid
David Mamet
Toni Morrison
Kenzaburo Oe
Richard Prince
Robert Rauschenberg
Nancy Rubins
Edward W. Said
Julian Schnabel
Saul Steinberg
William T. Vollmann
John Waters
Robert Williams

BUSINESS REPLY MAIL
First Class Mail   Permit No. 301   Denville, NJ

Postage will be paid by Addressee

GRAND STREET
Subscription Services
P.O. Box 3000
Denville, NJ 07834-9878

DESCANT

NOW IN ITS TWENTY-FIFTH YEAR

Isabel Allende
    Margaret Atwood
Catherine Bush
    Timothy Findley
Northrop Frye
    Douglas Glover
Katherine Govier
    Alberto Manguel
Eric McCormack
    Gwendolyn MacEwen
Josef Skvorecky
    Rosemary Sullivan
Jan Zwicky

25

THEMES

Filmsounds
Male Desire
First Nations
Space
Dis-Ease
Japan
The Book

Individuals $20; Institutions $35. Please
add $6 for subscriptions outside Canada

Descant: P.O. Box 314, Station P, Toronto, ON, M5S 2S8

THE AGE OF WIRE AND STRING

STORIES BY
Ben Marcus

"The most audacious literary debut in decades—

witty, startlingly inventive, funny

but fundamentally disturbing, language itself held together here by whimsical bits of wire and string. Ben Marcus is a one-of-a-kind phenomenon, a comic writer of exceptional power and originality."
—ROBERT COOVER

"A stream of pure oxygen"
—HARRY MATHEWS

Published by 🐎 Knopf

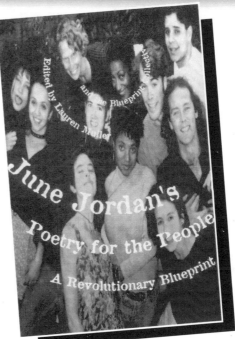

GRAND STREET

Egos

55

Front cover: Julian Schnabel, *Veramente Bestia V (girl with no eyes)*, 1988.
Back cover: Dennis Hopper, *Untitled*, 1995.

"Four Poems" by Shmuel HaNagid are excerpted from *Selected Poems of Shmuel HaNagid*, translated by Peter Cole. Copyright © 1996 by Princeton University Press. Printed by permission of Princeton University Press.

Grand Street (ISSN 0734-5496; ISBN 1-885490-06-2) is published quarterly by Grand Street Press (a project of the New York Foundation for the Arts, Inc., a not-for-profit corporation), 131 Varick Street, Room 906, New York, NY 10013. Contributions and gifts to Grand Street Press are tax-deductible to the extent allowed by law. This publication is made possible, in part, by a grant from the National Endowment for the Arts.

Second-class postage paid at New York, NY and additional mailing offices. Postmaster: Please send address changes to Grand Street Subscription Service, Dept. GRS, P.O. Box 3000, Denville, NJ 07834. Subscriptions are $40 a year (four issues). Foreign subscriptions (including Canada) are $55 a year, payable in U.S. funds. Single-copy price is $12.95 ($15 in Canada). For subscription inquiries, please call (800) 807-6548.

Grand Street is printed by Hull Printing in Meriden, CT. It is distributed to the trade by D.A.P./Distributed Art Publishers, 636 Broadway, 12th floor, New York, NY 10012, Tel: (212) 473-5119, Fax: (212) 673-2887, and to newsstands only by B. DeBoer, Inc., 113 E. Centre Street, Nutley, NJ 07110 and Fine Print Distributors, 6448 Highway 290 E., Austin, TX 78723. *Grand Street* is distributed in Australia and New Zealand by Peribo Pty, Ltd., 58 Beaumont Road, Mount Kuring-Gai, NSW 2080, Tel: (2) 457-0011.

GRAND STREET

Editor
Jean Stein

Managing Editor
Deborah Treisman

Art Editor
Walter Hopps

Assistant Editor
Jackie McAllister

Designer
Jim Hinchee

Editorial Assistant
Julie A. Tate

Administrative Assistant
Lisa Brodus

Interns
John Henderson
Caroline Linder
Christina Persico

Contributing Editors
Hilton Als, Dominique Bourgois, Colin de Land, Anne Doran,
Morgan Entrekin, Gary Fisketjon, Raymond Foye, Jonathan Galassi,
Stephen Graham, Barbara Heizer, Dennis Hopper, Hudson,
Andrew Kopkind (1935–1994), David Kornacker, Jane Kramer,
Erik Rieselbach, Edward W. Said, Robert Scheer, Elisabeth Sifton,
Jeremy Treglown, Katrina vanden Heuvel,
Gillian Walker, Drenka Willen

Publishers
Jean Stein & Torsten Wiesel

CONTENTS

This issue is dedicated to the memory of Terry Southern (1924–1995).

The Rear End Exists

L egend has it that when Josephine Baker hit Paris in the '20s, she "just wiggled her fanny and all the French fell in love with her." This achievement should be viewed in light of a deeper understanding, which is to say that there was a hell of a lot behind that wiggling bottom. Check it: Baker was from America and left it; African-Americans are on the bottom of the heap in America; we are at the bottom on the bottom, practically the bottom itself, and Baker rose to the top by shaking her bottom. Josephine Baker, bottom-shaker, does not merely "uncover . . . a new region for desire," is not simply a "Jazz Cleopatra,"* as her biographers have called her. Baker was American. Baker came from the bottom.

So, let us return to it.

bottom
BEhind
past tense
LedgeButt

Call me LedgeButt. When I was a kid they did. Not a term of endearment, of course. And to be sure uhhuhnn I cried. Mom tried to smooth things over: "Tuck," she counseled. To tuck meant to

---

* Quotations, unless otherwise marked, are taken from Phyllis Rose, *Jazz Cleopatra: Josephine Baker in Her Time* (New York: Doubleday, 1989).

stand straight—very straight—to try to hide the obvious promi-
nence of my back(ass)ward pointing bulb. Good kids are not badass.
There is the rump, and I was desperately American.

Tuck is counterpoint to *LedgeButt.* The rhythm of what it means
to be a good American: pulling in and moving upward (putting men
on the moon). America is past-free; we rely on a swift evaporation
of the what was. We move forward. And a protruding posterior is a
backward glance, a look which, in this country, draws no eyes. Has no
place. No rest.

See biography as geography—life story as stomping ground.
The body stands vertical and works as a mobile axis on which a world
turns, by which we navigate our wants. To be a good American you
straighten it up and don't look back. You tuck. But the buttock is
our largest muscle—larger than the heart. It is cleaved into two
halves, cupping us, much like parentheses. In its middle, an abyss.
At the abyss's center, the river's mouth: anus/eye, cyclops-like. Blood
in the stool means trouble. Insert a thermometer to learn the heat.
Biography is geography and the hide curves like a shy hillside. The
bear goes over the mountain. No, the bear, he *went*—past tense—
and bore it. What do we make of a country that denies us historical
referencing? Where can a consideration of the buttock(s) lead us?
Back back back tuh that—hide and seek. Now find thuh road but
there ain't no maps cause you weren't allowed tuh map none. What
do we make with the belief that the rear end exists?

The region still uncharted, much as this page.

So, here are some words:

 ass
 buttock(s)
 duff
 derriere
 keester
 behind
 BEhind
 yam
 blackside
 spanker
 main muscle (m&m)
 gluteus maximus

The buttock is meat. And with a meeting there's motion. *Gluteus maximus* is the largest of the three muscles which comprise this region, also the coarsest. It is perfectly positioned to give the region its name. To be named after your largest and coarsest is like being called LedgeButt. Baker crossed her eyes a lot. Knocking eye against eye: it's a look that looks backward and inward, behind. Little Ledge-Butt goes cross-eyed trying to recall her redeeming qualities (perhaps my rump once would have saved my life; Great Granny was a bustle-maker), and when none can be found, she invents them. Hot cross buns. A History: crossing your eyes to see it. Standing at a crossroads.

The telling and retelling of a story: "[Baker] told the story of her own life so many times and in so many different ways that one wonders what she was trying to get straight." Born in a country which denied her a historical referent, she sailed to France and starred in a Folie, this time far from home. Josephine made the most of her life, and made up most of it, too—not just her present and future but her past as well. She cleaved herself into two: *J'ai deux amours* was her theme song. She realized that there are two ways to couple a tattered past with a spangled present—by evolution or by mitosis—and she chose mitosis. Past and Present were separate but similar. Her early "ragamuffin" look matched her hometown; when she got glitter dresses her origins followed suit. Baker came from the bottom. The bottom cleaves and doubles, both bustle and bumper.

Josephine Baker was			saw rekaB enihpesoJ
not a good American			naciremA doog a ton
Her	BUTT	TTUB	reH
stuck out and She			ehS dna tuo kcuts
wanted it to stick			kcits ot ti detnaw
out more	SO	OS	erom tuo
She moved to France			ecnarF ot devom ehS

As Baker herself said: "The rear end exists. I see no reason to be ashamed of it. It's true that there are rear ends so stupid, so pretentious, so insignificant that they're good only for sitting on."

Call and response is a rear-ended activity—that is, there is no end to it. Etymology and mitosis are circular; evolution straight, linear.

Josephine fashioned her whole life like "a jazz improvisation, turning [it] inside out every few years." Repetition and revision in jazz *is* the writing. The life story is not so linear. In retelling hers, Baker was not trying to "get it straight" but to *get it round.* An A did not lead to a B but back to an A. The first scene in her life tableau, the Jorama*, is of Baker dancing; the last scene is the same, only time has changed. In jazz, a foundation is established as referent and then repeated and remade. Baker remade the referent itself: she jazzed up jazz. The truth has a certain sound (shape): it rings. The past tense of "hurt" is "hurt": a seamless conjunction. Cupping and uncupping hands hand out applause. You look like uh LedgeButt.

The buttocks meet like a clenched fist: Black Power! A beginning of things. An acceptance at bottom. Baker's cakes she got from her mother. A trait is a reference point to be remembered, and sometimes revised because a treasure, this booty, is often a burden. The German *Gift* is poisonous. The buttocks are heavy. Etymology and mitosis: Josephine the dancer invents a childhood in which her

---

*A wax museum of scenes from Baker's life that Baker opened at Les Milandes, her country home in the Dordogne, after her rise to celebrity.

dance-star mother Carrie encourages her to dance. In France a caged Zou-Zou* sings of home where she had a different cage. Watching Germans riot against her performances, she remembers the 1917 race riot in her hometown St. Louis, in which her people were run over a bridge and out of town. She becomes a French icon, a secret agent, a Civil Rights champion, a mother of twelve adopted children, a supporter of the Resistance; she shakes things up.

Begin again: where are you from?

> *You cant escape, theres nowhere to go . . . though*
> *your mind is somewhere else, your ass aint.*
>
> —*Amiri Baraka*

> *Josephine . . .*
> *of so many transformations i remember*
> *Josephine.*
>
> —*Jayne Cortez*

---

* *Zou-Zou* and *Princesse Tam-Tam*, two films starring Josephine Baker, were made in France in the mid '30s.

*You say kids today see Baker as a simple clown—a fool,
but I remember her as an adventuresome woman—cabaret per-
former and Civil Rights activist. And a humanitarian. Her like
were not allowed to achieve here. She went to France. She had to.
Like Robeson, Baldwin, DuBois, Wright, she had to leave. I also recall her—as—aahh—extremely beautiful. Did she wear fruit on
her head? No, around her waist. Fruit on her head was someone else.*

—*Mrs. Francis Parks and Mrs. Kathleen
Butler recall Josephine Baker.*

Here are some words:

    bustle
    fanny
    rump
    pratt
    hindquarters
    seat
    tuchas
    toosh
    heinie
    bottom
    bucket
    cakes
    cheeks
    crack
    buns (hot cross)
    yo-yo

The moon pulls us to it as do other places far away like Tim-
buktu, like France, like Africa: they draw us out like dreams. The
far-away provides a necessary distance, a new point of reference,
a place for perspective. Baldwin discovered what it meant to be
an American by going to France. Baker's love of France allowed her
to love America. Only when I leave the city am I from New York.
On the moon I am from earth. Dropping your dungarees you turn
assward to your looker. You bend slightly. You have mooned. Black
bottoms "eclipse." A gesture of daring which also demystifies.

Baker's bold bottom brought the rear to the forefront. She showed what holds the shithole. The hull of a ship. People in chains. A lunar eclipse can blind you.

The past has a shape which we place behind us—our posteriors, our posterity—and we move onward from it. In African religions there is less consideration of the future—that is, future means at most two years. The movement is into a past. Your short journey "forward" collects quickly behind you like the great mass in a "Khoi-Khoi" or "Hottentot"'s steatopygous buttocks. That collection is important. Baker makes a Folies entrance ass-first. With all that BEhind where you off to? Not nowhere too quickly. (A wrong move can set the race back ten years.) Josephine practiced her dance steps over and over so that even her wrong moves were the right moves. Harlem celebrated her with a Baker Day, 1927. The past, the shape of it. Separate but equal: behind, BEhind. Back of the bus. Back door. Back window for service. Young drudge Baker washes steps; la Baker bounds down front steps with leopard Chiquita in tow as onlookers wonder which animal is more wild. Separate but Equal? A new slavery. The future is as backward as the innovative dance in which she shakes her BEhind "like a little hummingbird." The hummingbird is a bird which flies backward (and hums while it flies). The future be-hind us. What charms can unlock it? Humming is wordless. Here are some words:

bootie
booTAY
posteriors
les fesses
bum
tail
rear end
Khoi-Khoi
kegba
Zou-Zou
Tam-Tam
sing song
caboose

Ham Bone, Ham Bone, where you been?
Round thuh worl n back uhgain!

Here is my journey's end, here is my butt.

—Othello

Poor old Michael Finnegan:
Begin-again!

Begin again. If the end is the end then the rear end (the end of the end) is the beginning. After Princess Tam-Tam whirls in night-clubs she returns home. Her donkey eats the book of civilization and fertilizes with it.

Josephine Baker died after opening her very successful come-back show in 1975—a show about the story of her life. Baker carried messages for the Resistance written in invisible ink on her sheet music; some of that ink, much information, is still invisible.

This Almost Last Day

Last final light,   rosy,
                         tenuous
under icicles,
                    a fire beginning
to spread & to fade at once,
                              offering
gift & threat together,   not
giving up,   not letting go,
                              reminding us—
faint saffron darkening to
pale tulip red—that it has not
forgone us.
                    This almost last day of
winter can only now begin to
expose what was hidden under
dead white,
dead gray,
                    so that a flush of whatever
flowers, what bears fruit,
                              what was buried under
a cold, a bitterness that drained,
that sapped our heat
                         is a sign now
of the roaring blaze filtered to us,
and even waking at night,   hearing
the rain metal-cold on
my shoulder, deep into my pillow,

I was not

lonely

(crying out, oh, oh

Nurse,   I saw him goe

O'r the white Alpes alone)

In the snows of the Arctic, the Antarctic,

what has

persisted under the whiteness, the crystal,

is blown out to us

(o my love is slaine)

is what we have always known.

All italicized quotations are from John Donne's *Elegie XVI on his Mystris.*

The Conversion
of St. Paolo Malfi

near Rome, 1995

The following is taken from a conversation between Julian Schnabel and Jean Stein, October 26, 1995.

What would you like to say about the paintings you have made in memory of Paolo Malfi?

These paintings were painted for a friend of mine who was killed this summer outside of Rome. He fell off his motorcycle and didn't really get hurt; then he took off his helmet and somebody ran him over in an Alfa Romeo while joyriding with his girlfriend. They dragged him three hundred meters before someone told them that there was something under the car.

We met about thirteen years ago, maybe a little longer than that. Paolo worked for Sandro Chia, then for Francesco Clemente, and he worked for me for a while and lived in my house in Bridgehampton for a few months in 1984. There was also an Austrian painter out there, who used to be a doctor, named Josef Ramaseder. So there were the Austrian doctor and the Italian philosopher; they'd walk around looking at the stars, reorganizing the chromosomes of the night sky.

Paolo was sort of an idiot savant who would make a cup of coffee for you. He wasn't a very talented painter but he was extremely inspired and he could tell you things about your paintings and about art that really rang true, things you would never think of. He loved painting more than anything else.

I don't know that there were any members of his family at the funeral. I know that Michele Zalopany and Cy's son, Alessandro Twombly, were there. I think Paolo's stay on this planet went almost unmarked. I believe art functions as a physical fact to commemorate the existence of being, like a tattoo. Maybe I lent him the body of these paintings for a while. I was always interested in the subject of the conversion of Saint Paul, and as I started to work this summer, I couldn't seem to do anything but paint the words "The Conversion of Saint Paolo Malfi, near Rome, 1995," or "La Conversion de Saint Paolo Malfi near Rome 1995," or "Il Conversion di San Paolo Malfi vicino Roma 1995." It's sort of a blend—written partly in Italian, partly in Spanish, partly in English, but Paolo's name is always spelled correctly. I am communicating with him through these paintings the only way I can.

Was Paolo Malfi a contemporary of yours? Could you describe him?

He was a little older than me. He probably would have been forty-five by now, but he looked very young. He had sad eyes and a bushy mustache and black curly hair. He looked like an extra in a Pasolini film.

Over what period of time did you make these paintings?

I painted them in the open air, in the morning and at the end of the day, at my studio in Montauk where I was also editing my movie on Jean-Michel Basquiat. It was probably from around July 25 to September 25.

Anyway, the last time I saw Paolo, we had a bowl of spaghetti together at the Bar Pitti on Sixth Avenue early last summer while I was scouting for my movie. He had made a relief that he traded for food with Giovanni, the owner of the restaurant. It was a small facade of a quaint Tuscan-looking building; but even though it was small, it didn't really fit anywhere, so it found its way next to some bottles on a glass shelf behind the bar. I guess it's still there.

I loved him very much; he was so gentle. He was always at Alba and Francesco Clemente's house, helping Alba when she was cooking something, or making a cup of coffee while extrapolating on the mating habits of a butterfly.

Untitled (Paolo Malfi), 1995.
Oil, gesso, resin, and banner on canvas dropcloth, 108 x 96 in.
p. 25

Untitled (The Conversion of St. Paolo Malfi), 1995.
Oil, resin, and print on tarpaulin, 108 x 96 in.
p. 26

Untitled (The Conversion of St. Paolo Malfi summer 1995 near Rome), 1995.
Oil and resin on tarpaulin, 120 x 108 in.
p. 27

Untitled (La Conversion de St. Paolo Malfi near Rome 1995), 1995.
Gesso, oil, and resin on canvas, 96 x 96 in.
p. 28

Untitled (The Conversion of St. Paolo Malfi near Rome), 1995.
Gesso, oil, and resin on canvas, 96 x 96 in.
p. 29

Untitled (La Conversion de San Paolo Malfi vicino Roma 1995), 1995.
Gesso, oil, and resin on canvas, 96 x 96 in.
p. 30

Untitled (The Conversion of St. Paolo Malfi near Rome), 1995.
Gesso, oil, and resin on canvas, 96 x 96 in.
p. 31

Untitled (Paolo Malfi), 1995.
Gesso, oil, resin, and banner on canvas dropcloth, 108 x 96 in.
p. 32

26

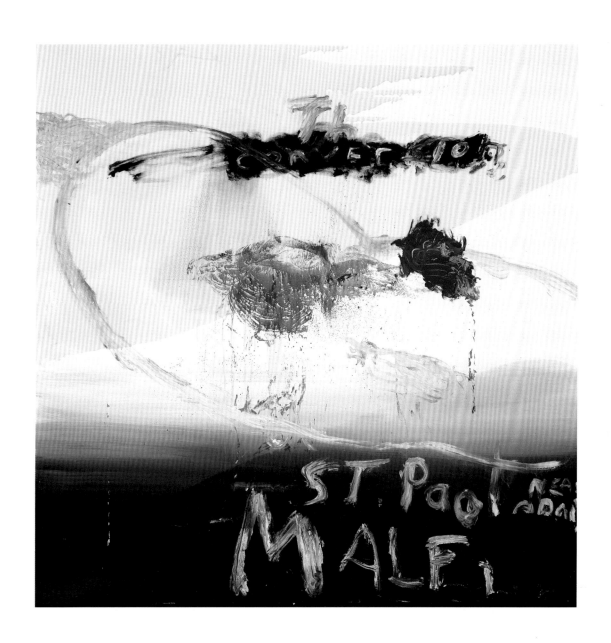

Paolo Malfi had two "mothers," Marietta and Mariuccia. He shuttled between them and then on to the friends, mentors, and wife who also "adopted" him. They all recognized in him a hidden gift, a secret illumination that he protected faithfully but was unable to express. Paolo Malfi was partially deaf, a stranger more comfortable abroad where his deafness could be mistaken for unfamiliarity with the local tongue.

Paolo picked apples in Calabria, was an electrician in majestic Tuscan churches, a gigolo in Düsseldorf; he lost his passport in Bombay, where he was thrown in jail and ate blades of grass. Later, he cooked papaya pizzas and sold them to Indian children at the historical ruins of Hampi. He set off on foot for the Himalayas and came back, his head swollen by sunstroke, unenlightened.

For $300, he bought a collection of eighteen Tanagra clay sculptures at a church sale in lower Manhattan. He found thirteen extremely rare, carved-wood oil jars from eighteenth-century Rajasthan on the corner of Bowery and East 3rd Street. He admired German painting and mourned the premature death of young American painter heroes. When he returned to Italy, he turned his talents to a curious trade: he produced paintings to be signed by famous, untalented actors, aging singers, or retired politicians, and then sold them as collectors' pieces to the sleepy but art-starved hinterland of industrial Europe. This trade amused Paolo and earned him a momentary prosperity. For all of his life, he was poor and relentlessly cultivated a sense of the sacred, at risk of appearing comical, troubled, or simply dumb.

After his tragic death in the summer of 1995, he appears as Saint Paolo Malfi in two dozen paintings by Julian Schnabel. In these works, flaming bold letters mark the passage of Time and Fate over that impassive surface of painting Paolo loved and knew so well.

•

Largeness is the substance and subject matter of Julian Schnabel's paintings. Largeness, seen from above, is immeasurable depth, the abyss. If we gaze at the sky, the very large tends toward infinity. Schnabel (playfully?) called one of his paintings *Portrait of God.* Maybe what is very large has to be very empty in order to contain that distance, the distance between us and what is beyond us.

Schnabel wants to prove to us, over and over again, that he knows what it takes to make a painting. He has reduced his vocabulary to a few arbitrary essentials: a tremulous line, a large glossy stain, a cloud of vivid color, a hard-edged stick-shape, a few words. Calmly he says, this is all: an illusionistic surface, precious and unflawed if seen from afar, puritanical and raw close up; colors in clear and bold contrast; few lines (only if they augment the sense of largeness); and other forms (only if borrowed and enlarged so as to lose their meaning).

Meanings enlarged become vaguer. The blurred edges of the largest truths awaken a sense of profound melancholy. Is there, in Schnabel's search for the "larger than life," a pathetic longing to revive the extinct lineage of history painters, from David to Twombly via Rivera? Or is it with tender irony that he celebrates on a monumental scale the pink blouse that his wife wore yesterday or the broken words overheard in the kitchen, where the Dominican maid is singing a Spanish song?

Julian would say: "I did not enlarge it. Think of the Egyptians: this is the scale of life (or at least of my own)." Ego enlarges itself ad infinitum in the freshly emptied shell of our new world: faceless powers have deprived us not only of a sense of history but of memory itself. Free from responsibility, unable to acknowledge one another, living icons of impotence and fragmentation, in our comfort, we lack nothing and share nothing, except the solitude of the dead, and, above all, their silence.

—Francesco Clemente

Othello Jr.

(One Moor Time)

$

=

"

A Ne(gr)o Classical Tragedy

of

"Amusement & Contempt"

*

The Prologue in Three Lowcoup

1.

AB, LHing on JEJ, Dig?

If James Earl Jones
   can play
   a Black Man

   Then don't complain
   about Laurence
   Olivier

   as
   O
Thell
   O,
       O.J.?

2.

Chris Darden

Othello & You
Othello Jr. too
All worked for
The Christians

& like them Jigs
you got the old
gig. In the arena
as entertainment for
Barbarians

Surrounded

by all of em's
Lyins

& yr boy
O Jr.
playing
Norman Bates

Making
 Faces
   &
     Screaming in Stares,

"You got my soul!
  I sold you my soul!"

"I'll kill to keep my Balls!"

3.

If O.J. is Othello
          Jr.

& Vermin
is Iago

Marsha Clarke
Desdemona

& Cato
doofus Cassio

Johnny C.
The Man

who ran out
on his father

Chris
    the
        Arena's Prey

    Preying
    for Civilization

    Then
    Othello was Called
to go out & greet
    Hell
    & Fight
    for it.

    In love with
    Gold
    Enthralled by
    Otherness!

But there is a
    Venice
    in California
Where the Punic Wars
    Rage on

    & there
    Moorish
        Women
        freed
        his
        Son!

A Mythical Topos:
A Dialogue

—April 26, 1995

JOHN NATHAN
As a very young man at Tokyo University in the late '50s, you published a series of stories which were astonishing in the originality of their language and the freshness of their vision. Many who read those stories, in their youth in Japan, still remember their impact. You managed to capture the complex confabulation of betrayal, anger, despair, and hope that your entire generation experienced, growing up in Japan in the post–World War II period. A huge readership hung on your every word for a period of twelve to fifteen years. Since then, you have continued to grow at an alarming rate, you have read and deepened and become more and more complex. And that has cost you some of your readership in your own country. Despite your mounting isolation, you have continued your meticulous and ceaseless examination of the self, of moral responsibility, and of the relationship of the individual to post-war society. Your readers have, in some measure, been unable to keep up with you. That is to say, you have made demands which some of them have not been able to fulfill.

KENZABURO OE
My way of writing is always to write a very natural text, and then begin to change it, twist it, and turn it upside down. I do everything unnaturally. That is how I created my famous anti-Japanese—or anti–classical Japanese—style. When I was twenty-eight, my son Hikari was born with a brain impairment. I believe this experience

changed me very deeply. Before his birth, I was writing very conceptually, so I exaggerated many things and I believe that is a weakness of the novels I wrote then. But I improved myself after the birth of my son. I believe that my later books are written more creatively, more productively.

I gave a lecture at Harvard University almost thirty years ago, and a very important person in the audience, Dr. Reischauer, stood up and said something I have never forgotten. "Mr. Oe," he observed, "I can agree with almost all of what you have said. There is, however, one thing I cannot accept." Tension mounted in me and in the audience. Dr. Reischauer, as you know, had been the United States ambassador to Japan in the 1960s. He had been assaulted by Japanese youths and had undergone a slow recovery from the attack. This comment came shortly after he had returned to academic work. "You mentioned," he continued, "that the imaginative power of Japanese politicians has weakened. But I think, and I speak from experience, that Japanese politicians had no imagination to begin with."

JOHN NATHAN   When I was a student of Professor Donald Keene's at Columbia University, he often used an Italian expression which means, "To translate is to traduce." Chapter 10 of *A Personal Matter*, which I translated, begins, "They were watching the midnight news, Bird in bed on his stomach, lifting only his head, like a baby sea urchin." Some years after this translation had come out, and had been locked onto the page, I accused you of using sloppy imagery—because, of course, a baby sea urchin has no head. And you said, "I never wrote such a thing." I, in the hubristic mode that was my style in those days, said, "I'm certain that you wrote it." I pulled the Japanese and English versions from your bookshelf, showed them to you, and said, "You see, I'm right."

KENZABURO OE   At the time of the conversation, you and I were sitting with a very great American journalist, who was writing a critique. The journalist asked you, "How can a sea urchin lift his head?" You answered, "Japanese people eat a lot of fish and sea products. We cannot imagine how dedicated the Japanese people are to studying the movements of sea animals—to the extent that every ordinary Japanese can perceive the very delicate movement of a baby sea urchin."

**JOHN
NATHAN**

I believe we were alone, but you have now created a new legend, a third person present. A magnificent example of an artist transforming reality with the power of his imagination, something you have stood for for thirty years. For you, this event has the reality of a dream.

We looked at the book and of course what you had written was "kowani," with the Katakana "wa,"—which means baby alligator. And the difference between that "wa" and the "u" of "uni" is one tiny vertical eyelash which I had misread the first time I read the book, and misread hundreds of times subsequently, and so I read "kouni" instead of "kowani" and translated "baby sea urchin."

To continue with the problem of translation: In your new trilogy, *Flaming Green Tree*, which is a powerful and important summation of the world you have built, one of the characters constantly brings William Butler Yeats's poetry into the story. When a Japanese reader reads Yeats in your work, is he reading your translation of Yeats?

**KENZABURO
OE**

Yes, when I quote poems—Yeats, Dante, William Blake, or Malcolm Lowry—I always translate them myself.

**JOHN
NATHAN**

Thus, your translation of Yeats is part of your Japanese text. But the translator into English would have to return your translation of Yeats to the original Yeats. When the English reader experiences Kenzaburo Oe translated into English and the original William Butler Yeats, the balance is profoundly affected. I assume that the goal of translation is to create the same impact on the English reader that you want to create on the Japanese reader. So is it not different if I turn your translation of Yeats into the real Yeats? When I translate, should I take the Yeats and in some way reconstitute it?

**KENZABURO
OE**

When I translate a poem, the two texts always coexist. I hope that when I translate Yeats, the reader hears some of the music of the original. Static imagination is not imagination. Real imagination is always moving and deepening and I hope to evoke some movement, some vacillation, to use Yeats's word, between the original and my translation.

The word "vacillation" is very important in Yeats's poems. Yeats believed in the coexistence of two poles. We are always vacillating. That is our life. And if we want to be poets or novelists, we must always vacillate between these two points. I hope to continue that vacillation until the end of my life.

I believe that Kobo Abe and Yukio Mishima were the two geniuses of the century in Japanese literature. Kobo Abe was a very dynamic genius. He maintained the movement, the vacillation, until his death. But Mishima was not a man who vacillated and he committed suicide very young, at forty-five. His style is static. Beautiful but static. If you want to live a continuous creative life, you cannot maintain a static style. Even a genius like Mishima could only maintain his static style for twenty years or so.

I have said that I am going to give up writing fiction. Very honestly speaking, what I am going to give up is the story-telling narrative. I have continuously written in a narrative style and I think it is my weakness. So, for the last ten years or so of my life, I hope to find a new form of expression. I am already trying to find it. One of the reasons for this is that I hope to do something that will affect Japanese society more directly. This is the most important problem in my life and literature right now.

JOHN NATHAN Yeats was central to your last work. And in an earlier book of yours, *Journey to the Lost Years*, you had the hero, a Dante specialist, continually invoking the world of the Inferno and Paradise. Before that, you used William Blake in your book *Rouse Up O Young Men of the New Age*. I have an example here from the final chapter:

> "Eeyore, dinner's ready," I called to him. "Come on, sit down." But Eeyore's eyes never moved from the record player. And then the muscles in his broad, manly shoulders tensed.
>
> And he said, as though announcing a considered decision, *"Eeyore won't be coming. Since Eeyore isn't here anymore altogether. Eeyore won't be coming over there."*
>
> I could feel my wife watching me as I looked down at the table. The sense of loss assaulting me was so unequivocal I didn't think I could handle her gaze. What had happened just now? Had it actually happened, and would it go on? I managed to keep tears from my eyes, but I could feel myself flush from my cheeks to my ears.
>
> "Eeyore, no way! You've come home so of course you're here!" His younger sister's voice was gentle, soothing, but Eeyore remained silent.

"He'll be twenty in June, maybe he doesn't want to be called Eeyore anymore," his younger brother said. "I bet he wants to be called by his real name—that's what they must be using at the dorm!"

An unhesitating activist once he takes a logical stand, Eeyore's brother crossed the room and said, squatting at his side, "Hikari, let's eat. Mom's made all your favorites!"

"That should be fine. Thank you," Eeyore replied. . . .

Shoulder to shoulder despite the large difference in their height and girth, the two brothers came to the dining table. So this is it? I thought to myself as I watched them begin to attack their food, still feeling the shock of loss I had received a minute before, no more calling him Eeyore? The time was ripe, I supposed. My son, the time has surely come for us to cease calling you by your infant name of Eeyore and to begin calling you Hikari! You have arrived at that age. Before long, you, my son Hikari, and your younger brother, Sakurao, will stand before us as young men. Lines from Blake's preface to *Milton*, verses I had read aloud time and time again, seemed to surge up in me: "Rouze up O Young Men of the New Age! Set your foreheads against the ignorant Hirelings! For we have Hirelings in the Camp, the Court & the University: who would if they could, for ever depress Mental & prolong Corporeal War." With Blake as my guide, I beheld a phantasm of my sons as young men of a new Age, a baleful atomic Age which would require them the more urgently to set their foreheads against the ignorant Hirelings—and I could assuredly feel myself at their side, re-born as another Young Man, hearing, grown elderly in time and having to endure death's agony, the words proclaimed by the voice from the "Tree of Life" in encouragement to all Humankind as though they were spoken to me and for me: "Fear not Albion unless I die thou canst not live/But If I die I shall arise again & Thou With me."

This is, in a sense, a very Christian configuration or construct. And I notice that when you translated Blake, you began with "Albion"—Blake's word for Everyman—and left out the words "Christ said." How do you, Kenzaburo Oe, relate to these Christian notions of redemption and rebirth? Are you yourself playing with something that is related to Christianity?

KENZABURO OE I don't think the metaphorical images in William Blake's work are what we would call authentically Christian. His symbolism is not Christian only—it also dates from the tradition before Christianity. In my translation of *Jerusalem*, Christ is on the Tree of Life, but the meaning of this Tree of Life is not entirely Christian. This Christ says to Albion, a human being, "If I don't die, you cannot live on, on the day of redemption. I am with you." This concept is also not authentically Christian. I use the metaphor and symbolism of William Blake, especially from his *Prophesies*, but I am using them from the side of tradition.

Creating myths and modifying and deconstructing myths is the most important technique of my literature. My village, on Shikoku Island, is surrounded by dense forests and cut off from the other villages. So the villagers have created many village myths and much of my writing is based on those myths. Even today, my villagers continue to create new myths, especially my mother, who is ninety-three years old. She is the toughest mythmaker. Recently, I asked my sister, "How is my mother? Is she weak these days?" And my sister said, "Your conception of human beings is very simple. Your mother is not that kind of woman." Her new myth is: "My third son went to Atlanta. He was invited by the Atlanta Olympic Organization." I was invited with Derek Walcott, Toni Morrison, and Octavio Paz to the 1995 Assembly of the Atlanta Cultural Olympiad—but my mother cut the word "Cultural" out of the title. She told the villagers: "My son was invited to the Atlanta Olympics. He is now sixty years old. You know, ladies and gentlemen, my third son is a very weak person. His body is very, very shabby. But my son went to Tokyo and he created a new body. . . ." Then she told the villagers—and they believed it—"Oh, Kenzaburo Oe became very strong, after a long, long training of his body. Now, at sixty years old, he won a race . . ." Soon the villagers will forget whether I went to Atlanta in 1995 or 1996. "So at the beginning of the twenty-first century, my son will become the medal winner of the Atlanta Olympic Games." This is the kind of myth she creates. And she expects people at the beginning of the twenty-first century to believe it. She believes in the continuity of human beings. She believes in their history and maintains hope for the future. I was born in this village, so I must create myths where others speak the truth.

But I also believe that there is no distinct difference between "truth" and "myth." Fundamentally, I don't believe there is nonfiction. If something is written, it is fiction. That is the role of language. I think that nonfiction writers in the U.S. are the most productive and talented; but do you believe that when Norman Mailer writes about the Oswald case, he is writing nonfiction? Nonfiction is just another kind of fiction.

For a long time, Japanese literature didn't create any new myths. We have the classical myths of the sixth and seventh centuries, but after that our myths were taken over by our emperor-system cultural structure and we lost the power to create new ones. Our literature was weakened by this for almost a thousand years. Then, over a period of almost a hundred and twenty years, through the modernization of Japan, Japanese writers created the "I-novel," *shishosetsu.* We always write about ourselves, so we think that we are not writing fiction.

In the hope of liberating myself from this form, I generally begin by writing about my life, about my family, then I change completely to the dimension of pure fiction, using the European concept. If you compare my work with Japanese I-novels and with John Cheever's work, I believe you'll find that I am much closer to John Cheever in technique.

JOHN NATHAN
You have created a mythical topos in your work, places with very distinct geographical features: the hollow, the bamboo grove, the inlet where you lie privately in the river. One begins to learn your map. Accompanying that map are various myths which have incredible reality and magical power; some of them you may have actually heard, and most of them, I suspect—although it doesn't matter—you made up. In your new trilogy, the second volume of which is called *Vacillation* after the Yeats poem, you talk about the power of place and its importance to the novelist. You create an "Uncle K," who is of course Kenzaburo Oe, and set him in a village on the periphery of Japan, with clear geographic richness and tonality. Is that your way of establishing an authentic identity for Kenzaburo Oe? Does that anchor you?

KENZABURO OE
The power of place is very important. I think it is the first condition of the novel. I said that Japanese myths become very weak after the

seventh or eighth century, but Japanese folklore maintains a vivid and original power of imagination. And Japanese folklore is always very conscious of the power of place. For instance, I believe you know Japan's most famous folktale, *Momotaro* or *Peach Boy*.

Once upon a time, there was an old man and an old woman. This is a very simple and not-so-structural beginning. But the next line is structural and complicated. *The old man went to the mountain to get firewood.* A place appears, and an upward orientation. Then, the most important line, the third line, with a downward orientation: *The old woman went to the river to wash.* Upward and downward movement, and the river is horizontal. So now there is a place. And a river that leads to other places, mystical, unknown places, and comes from other mystical, unknown places. A horizontal line, a vertical line, and up comes the place. Then the Peach Boy comes from the horizontal upward, from some place with power. And he comes in a big peach, *donburiko.* The couple cuts the peach open and the Peach Boy comes out. He becomes a big, beautiful young man and he lives very happily with the old man and old woman. Then he goes downward through the horizontal. When he gets to the unknown, mysterious place, he fights with a monster and returns with something from the monster. He gets married. Then the old man dies and the Peach Boy becomes an old man. So the new old man goes to the mountain, and the new old woman goes to the river.

I have studied this Peach Boy folktale for a long time. I began when I was three years old and I continue to study it. So when you say you suspect the authenticity of my places, you are right. Yes, I have created new myths, new places, new peoples, a new history. I have made a fictional structure. Then, through this fictional structure, I have thought about the real problems of Japanese culture and politics, about everything in Japan or in the world.

I cannot say that literature can affect society very effectively. But it cannot be free from society or reality either. Every writer bases his novels on reality and also directs them toward reality. I am criticized for having left the real political scene. But I don't think that I have: if I write about William Blake, I do so to shed light on today's society. I hope to do something real through my literature.

From *J*

It had been one minute since the crowded subway train had pulled out of the Diet Station. J and the old man both noticed the young man at the same time. He was about eighteen, well-built, and wore an English trench coat—the kind meant for young people, with clusters of buttons and buckles. Peering out from the collar of his coat, his sweat-drenched face and neck had a white glow. J and the old man saw one of the young man's legs as he took a determined step into the densely packed thicket of human bodies. For an instant they saw his bare calf and knee. He was wearing deerskin boots. He seemed thin, but his fleshy neck and head suggested that his weight was well above average. If he looked thin, it was probably because, apart from the trench coat and boots, he was completely naked.

The subway train was racing along at top speed, shaking like a newspaper boy late for his rounds on a winter morning. The boy took another step forward. Beads of sweat surfaced on his forehead like fish eggs. His body was now fitted snugly against the back and buttocks of a young girl. She had a monstrous growth on her forehead and a smug, upturned nose, but he had approached her from behind. With steely self-control, he sighed quietly, soundlessly, and glanced cautiously around. He had the eyes of a dog too sick even to chase a sewer rat. The fever had erased whatever glimmer of cunning vitality those eyes might still have contained. His small nose,

Mongolian in shape, widened heroically as he sniffed for any suspicious scent. About fifteen feet above the passengers' heads lay the bleak evening city in early winter. Ten million people lived there and the young man seemed to know that there was not one who would help him in his very personal mission.

He seemed at ease, although dripping with sweat. In his arrogance, he felt completely removed from the world around him. He was deliriously excited, almost fatally aroused, as he let his hard male weapon emerge from a small slit in a hidden pocket of his coat. He began to rub it lovingly, anxiously, determinedly, against the girl's buttocks through her orange coat; and an innocuous, saintly smile began to curl on his lips, then spread gradually across his entire face. . . .

J and his elderly but well-built friend stood shoulder to shoulder as they watched this scene. The tension was so unbearable that both felt an urge to close their eyes. The old man was afraid he'd have a heart attack. The train pulled into the next station and stopped, disgorged some people, sucked in others, and started again. Hoping the boy had disappeared, J and the old man looked toward the place where he'd been standing. The jungle of passengers was less dense than before, but they discovered the young man still in action. To make matters worse, he was about to have an orgasm, as inevitable as death itself. Suddenly, not only J and his friend, but everyone on the train, seemed to open their eyes wide and focus on the young man with a terrible, united force. Under this glare of strangers' eyes, he climaxed. At that moment, a powerfully built middle-aged man, who'd been standing next to J and the old man, reached out and grabbed the collar of the young man's trench coat as if he were about to rip it off his back. J and the old man swallowed hard and sighed.

"He went too far," J whispered in the old man's bulbous ears.

The two realized sadly that a squid-like ink of shame and fear was already clouding the pool of pleasure in the boy's loins, as despair imposed its faint moan and shiver onto the final gasp of orgasm. Their hearts raced. They were sure that the *chikan's** entrails would twist like so much rope when he realized that he was cornered, with no chance of escape. They knew he was imagining himself, his

---

* Literally, an oversexed idiot, generally used to refer to subway molesters.

trench coat torn off, dragged naked to the police like a masturbating chimpanzee, with his eyes no bigger than wrinkles and his sodden penis dripping. The jelly of his semen, the color of tears, had already congealed, stiffening his crotch, as he stood before those countless hostile eyes.

"A real desperado, a true *chikan*," J said passionately. "Aren't we going to help him?"

"Yes, let's rescue him if we can," the old man answered. Side by side they approached the man who had caught the youth. They were pale with excitement, as if they were the ones being rescued.

"We'll give him to the police, the rotten *chikan*," the old man said to the indignant man who was holding him. The old man's cheeks were stiff with tension, but he finally managed a slight smile and tried to soften his glittering eyes, which were glazed like a hawk's. The captor looked like a firefighter, but J's friend's imposing physique didn't compare unfavorably. Gently but firmly, the older man overcame the younger one. The old man's physical bearing had always fascinated J, and he felt vaguely jealous of the masses of muscle he must have had in his thirties. But J—and J only—could also see that the blades of dissatisfaction were solidly planted in this wild old bull and could not be shaken out.

"A pervert like this deserves a good beating, doing that to an innocent girl!" The self-righteous citizen began to overact.

The wrinkled skin around the old man's eyes was the color of dead leaves, but in an instant of fierce anger, he blushed. The other, mistaking the old man's anger for sympathy with his own indignation, gave him a good-natured nod. J noted how the old man's face, red with anger, resembled the boar on the Gordon's Gin label—it was a resemblance he had noticed the day he first met the old man.

J intervened before the old man got out of hand. "We'll hand him over to the police. If you'll give me your card, we'll let the chief know that it was really you who caught him."

"It is a pleasure to meet people like you who believe in justice. If I had the time, I'd go to the police with you. The damned *chikan*!" the middle-aged man said. He took a creased old business card from the wallet in his inside pocket and handed it to J.

The old man and J held their captive from both sides. They felt him trembling against their sides and hips. "Don't cry, and don't be so stupid as to scream or beg," J whispered in a voice which sounded only in the back of his throat, as the boy shook silently with his eyes downcast. His opponent was comforting the sobbing girl whose orange coat was stained. When he tried to wipe the semen off with his mouse-gray handkerchief, the girl started to scream again. She was pale and seemed about to vomit up bile. The passengers who'd gathered around them laughed in happy and excited voices. For J, seeing this hurt, ugly girl was the only thing that made him feel slightly repelled by the boy. Why had he rubbed his penis against a girl who was so repulsive and self-righteous and, at the same time, so miserably frightened?

"Listen, miss, this sort of thing won't get you pregnant and you haven't lost your virginity. You are still pure," the man whispered to the girl. His efforts to win himself further glory made the other passengers laugh again. Only now did J and the old man realize that the girl's benefactor smelled of alcohol.

At the next station, the old man and J took the boy's arms and stepped down onto the platform. When the door closed, the departing man waved and smiled, baring his teeth like a monkey. They looked like yellow grains of Indian corn. J tore up the man's business card and threw it away. Then, he turned to the train and, deadly serious, pulled down his lower eyelid to show him the red eye of contempt. Without waiting to see the man's reaction, J and the old man took the boy's arms again (they looked, now, like three generations of a happy family). As they followed the platform to the stairs, J and the old man took turns giving him advice.

"Your methods are a total mess. It'd be a wonder if you didn't get caught. Why aren't you a little more careful?"

"Besides, you're looking for trouble if you don't do it when there are more people on the train. If you want that kind of excitement, you have to do it when the train is packed."

The old man and J dropped the boy's arms, stopped, and let him continue walking. The rescue had succeeded. Even though he was free, the young man took two or three more steps in the same posture, as if still restrained. Then he paused abruptly and turned around, looking at the old man and J suspiciously. His small nose was no longer bulging, and his eyes were no longer those of a sick dog. The physical serenity that comes after orgasm had given an angelic look to his large face. He looked like a dying martyr after an ordeal, a saint whose sufferings had ended.

"You guys are letting me . . . ?" he asked in a shrill voice. He was unsure, ready to run at any moment.

"No, we're not going to turn you over to the police. That was just a stupid joke," J stammered, as if admitting something difficult. The boy was so serious that his rescuers almost felt ashamed of themselves.

"Today I'd made up my mind to get caught. I wanted to suffer. I meant it, and I went to the point of no return," he said. It was a kind of challenge.

J and the old man looked at each other amazed. When J saw his friend finally manage a smile, he reluctantly smiled himself. It was the smile of a magnanimous boxer who appreciates the strength of his opponent after being fooled by a quick punch to his weak spot. Both were now curious and they gave the boy a more careful look. There was something irritated and resentful about him, but also something sad. The post-orgasmic calm, which had given him the appearance of a gentle saint a few moments before, had disappeared, and the dark shadow of an extremely sharp discontent had replaced it.

"I'm not wearing anything but this coat and these boots. I really suffered before I finally made up my mind to go out like this. And making that final leap into pleasure, with everyone watching me, was like closing my eyes and letting go of the handlebars when I'm on a bike doing eighty. I'm like a member of a suicide squad, and you guys turn me into a game?"

Tears filled his bloodshot eyes. Suddenly he threw a punch at J, who ruthlessly blocked his forearm, using the boxing techniques he'd learned in college. Groaning in pain, the boy dropped his arms limply and cried a little.

"If you like, we can still hand you over to the subway guards or the police," J threatened. Panting, he glared at the boy and rubbed his wrists, which were starting to turn red.

"That won't be necessary," the boy said. His bleary eyes seemed frightened again.

J saw that the boy was very agitated and emotionally unbalanced, as if he had taken sleeping pills and had yet to fall asleep. This could have been due to some new drug that J didn't know about, but it reminded him of the terribly appealing German sleeping drug to which he had become hopelessly addicted several years earlier. It was the drug J's first wife had used to kill herself. After she stopped breathing that night, J had been desperate, but he finally fell into the depths of the fearful unconscious. . . .

J's memories took over and dissipated his anger at the boy trying to hit him. Finally, J was smiling.

One morning, J had decided to become a *chikan*. He had felt very far from the sexual world and had wanted an anti-sexual form of self-punishment, as it were. At the same time, he was driven by a certain sexual excitement, a violent hunger. But at the time of that first conversion he wasn't really aware of the two-headed sex monster that lived inside him. One early winter morning at nine o'clock, still in bed after a sleepless night, he had simply thought to himself, *I want to be a chikan.* He'd walked from the bedroom into the main room that his wife used as a work space. She was discussing the script of her new film with her partner, the cameraman.

"You can use the Jaguar if you like," he said, "I'm going to take the train."

"Where are you going?" his wife and the cameraman asked. He said it didn't matter as long as he went by train. So began J's daily routine of roaming the city. Early each morning he left the apartment. Late at night he returned. Usually he found his wife sleeping on the couch in the work space, exhausted, with a blanket drawn up to her chest. Sometimes they barely spoke for days at a time.

Why had he chosen to be a *chikan*? J had never really given it much thought—somewhere in his heart, he was continually aware that he was not yet truly deviant. On the other hand, he realized that, when he finally found himself humiliated in the strong grip of an angry stranger, he would have no choice but to think it through. And at times, in the depths of his being, a flash of what it meant to be a *chikan* would rise flickering to the surface of his consciousness, like a sudden stay of execution.

One evening J was riding the outbound express from the Tokyo Station on the National Railways Chuo Line. Standing immediately in front of him was a woman of about his age. She was at a right angle to him, and their bodies were pressed together, with her chest, stomach, and thighs fitted to his. J caressed the woman. His right hand moved into the space between her buttocks, while his left hand traveled down her belly toward the space between her thighs. His erect penis was touching the outside of her leg. He and the woman were about the same height. His heavy breath stirred the down on her flushed earlobes. At first J trembled with fear and his breathing was irregular. Was the woman not going to cry out? Would she not seize his arms with her two free hands and call for help from the people around them? When his fear was at its peak, J's penis was hardest. Now it was pressed tightly against the woman's thigh. He shook with profound fear as he stared straight at her chiseled profile. Her low, unwrinkled forehead, the bridge of her short, upturned nose, the large lips below a layer of coffee-colored down, the firm jaw, the splendid, dark eyes, cloudy and almost black. She barely blinked at all. As J caressed her rough woolen skirt, he suddenly seemed to lose consciousness. If the girl cried out in disgust or fear, he would have an orgasm. He held on to this fantasy like fear, like desire. But she didn't cry out. She kept her lips firmly closed. Suddenly her eyes closed tightly, like a curtain falling to the stage. At that instant the restraining pressure of her buttocks and thighs relaxed. Descending, J's right hand reached the depths of her now-soft cheeks. His left hand went to the hollow between her outspread thighs.

J lost his fear and, at the same time, his desire weakened. Already his penis was beginning to wilt. He persisted with his caresses out of curiosity and a sense of duty. He became coolheaded. *This is what always happens*, he thought. *When you can get away with anything, you can never get to that one reality that transcends this condition.* It was nothing more than a step in the same process that had repeated itself time and again since the day he had decided to become a *chikan*, a deviant. Then, suddenly, his fingertips felt the orgasm of this stranger.

A moment later, the train rumbled into Shinjuku Station. J saw the big glistening tears that slipped out from between the woman's tightly shut eyelids rise steadily, break, and run down her cheeks. Her lips were pursed as if she'd bitten into a green plum, carving deep wrinkles that could have been cracks all around her mouth. But at that moment the doors opened and J was pushed out of the car by the human wave, away from the woman and onto the platform. After the train left, he continued to stand on the platform. *She didn't look at me for even a second*, he thought, and he felt so terribly lonely that tears came to his eyes, as they had to hers. He thought of his overwhelming loneliness and fear on the night his first wife had taken sleeping pills and killed herself. He and his wife had been sleeping cheek to cheek. The drug had put her into a deep sleep, and she was snoring loudly. But even in her sleep she was still crying and her tears had awakened him. He knew it was a ridiculous idea, but J thought that if he could meet the woman on the train again, he would want to marry and live with her, even if he had to beg her. For several weeks, at the same time of day, toward evening, he watched out for her at Tokyo Station. But he'd already lost any distinct memory of her looks. It was only the shape and the color and the glistening and falling of her tears that he remembered clearly.

His single encounter with that woman was J's happiest memory as a *chikan*. His dark, unhappy memories were countless. In the early days, all he did in the trains and the buses, in the department store elevators, was stand petrified and immobilized, pale and dripping with sweat, as he burned with the desire for action. From the time he left his apartment in early morning until late at night, he roamed ceaselessly, like the Flying Dutchman, from one end of Tokyo to the other, but he was unable actually to touch the body of a stranger. That period lasted for several weeks. The day that J became an anti-social activist—in the form of a *chikan*, a molester—he also became extraordinarily sensitive to the presence of society. He discovered all of its various taboos, traps, and restraints; never in his life had he felt this larger society rise up against him with such clamorous self-assertion. People who saw him on the street during that period no doubt believed that he was a man of incomparably firm morals. In those days, J was still in the painful period of apprenticeship. . . .

Some of the social icons that aroused fear in J were the advertisements posted on the ceilings of the trains. If one of those ads bore the words "Encyclopedia for 80 Million," J would feel like an outlaw warlord launching an attack on the eighty million citizens of Japan who loved their encyclopedias. He would begin to shiver with the excitement of battle. At such times, the milk-white grips of the train straps, all swaying in unison, were nooses waiting to choke him. He would break out in a sweat and close his eyes.

Even after he'd survived those dark weeks and learned to act freely as a *chikan*, he wasn't always happy. To be a loner in a crowd of strangers, stealthily touching their sexual parts, then escaping safely: that ideally perverse achievement, he thought, must be impossible to enact perfectly. He dreamt of a hunter entering a forest of wild

animals, killing a deer, and then leaving it there. The hunter leaves
the forest exhausted, but he has tasted a stoic, manly exaltation.
When J did battle in the forest of strangers on a rush-hour train and
retreated again, he was hoping for that hunter's exaltation, but he
almost always faltered halfway and was left dissatisfied, irritated, and
humiliated, or he was filled with a useless hatred and found himself
indulging in unbridled excesses. . . .

One evening J was standing on a large bus that had started from
Shibuya. His right hand held the strap, and his left was pressed from
behind against the naked skin of a large woman, between her stock-
ings and corset. He was staring straight at the abundant, heavy hair
on her massive head, just inches from his eyes. As he smelled her
hair, the tension and excitement made his throat so dry it hurt. To
hide the fact that he'd raised the woman's heavy woolen skirt, he was
crouching forward with his knees thrust out in front of him, like
somebody riding a horse. In this position, it was difficult for him to
hold his left hand on the woman's naked thigh. He felt an irritating
pain that numbed his arm from his left shoulder to his fingertips,
but he endured the pain without moving. Then the woman suddenly dropped her hips as if to lean over and rested her weight on
J's unstable left hand. He lost his balance and his head bumped hard
against the woman's shoulder. When he managed to stand back up,
his left hand was caught firmly in the woman's powerful hand. He was
stunned, and began to spin around, to spiral down into a maelstrom
of fear. When the bus came to the next stop, the woman pulled him
by the hand through the crowd of passengers and off the bus. He
was pale and covered with sweat. His heart was soiled with his own fear
and despair, but at the same time he felt some kind of deeper,
preordained harmony. It was then he realized for the first time that
a desire for self-punishment was part of his fervid lust for the pleasures of a *chikan*. He didn't try to escape. Rather, he walked where the
woman led him, like a boy with his mother, to the most contemptu-
ous, cruel policeman of all. But the woman didn't take J to the
police. She took him to a room in a cheap hotel, where the walls and
ceiling and floor were layered with cardboard to deaden the sound.
He tried his best to put an end to his humiliating sexual service as
quickly as possible, but he was impotent to the last. The woman lay
down in the ugly light of the fluorescent lamp and closed her eyes
as if in anguish. Her naked body was covered with yellow fat and

looked like the larva of a wasp. She didn't speak, didn't move. J was naked beside her. He pulled up his knees and dropped his head flaccidly. He was in despair. He felt as though the only thing living and moving in that room was the smell of their two naked bodies. Finally he also closed his eyes, and sat huddled and motionless. Offering no resistance, he waited for those hundred years of hell to pass. The woman didn't move either. She was a fox playing dead. It was as if her body was putrefying even as she lay there.

In a crowd, touching a woman's sex beneath her underwear for even an instant excited him to the point where he was ready to risk his entire existence. But when he and the owner of that sex were skin to skin, all of his sexual instincts worked to refuse her. This he understood from such bitter experiences as this one. He was in a constant state of dissatisfaction, but for several months he hadn't had intercourse, even with his wife. Wistfully seeking the slightest opportunity for sexual contact, he became part of the city's crowd of strangers, roaming from morning until late at night. Until the day he met the old man, he had felt utterly alone, more alone than he had ever felt in his life. If he hadn't chanced to meet him, J probably would have become an explosively dangerous deviant, a true *chikan*, and would already have been arrested. In that sense, he felt blessed by the relationship of mutual assistance that he and the old man had established. . . .

J was on the Yamanote Line, planning to make a circuit of Tokyo. It was close to the end of morning and a faint winter sun was shining. Almost all the seats in the car were occupied but nobody was standing. The floor was like the gray-black back of a mouse, and dust was rising from it into the sunlight. The passengers were bored, but not so tired as to be distracted. It was a bad moment for a *chikan*.

The situation changed when the train pulled into Ueno Station. A group of about twenty laughing high-school girls entered J's car. Their teacher had probably just taken them to see the mummies or the Jomon Pottery at the museum. J promptly rose from his seat and made his way into the throng of girls, searching for the most advantageous position for a *chikan*, but before he could get there, he saw a tall old man get up from his seat. The man moved with real agility, but behaved as though nothing unusual was happening. J had a premonition and, his heart pounding, he watched. The old man was well built and imposing. In his luxurious camel overcoat, his large chest and broad shoulders towered over the swarm of schoolgirls' heads. He had a white silk scarf tied around his thick neck, and a soft hat pulled down over his head. Except for the skin on his face, which was covered with wrinkles the color of dead leaves, and his eyes, which were keen like those of a bird of prey, he was the ideal image of old age, the man you see clutching a golf club in ads for health tonics. Looking at him made you feel better. It let you nurse illusions about your own old age. The high-school girls saw several empty seats, but didn't move to sit down. They stood talking with their bodies pressed tightly together, like a herd of zebras threatened by a lion or a flock of scared chickens. Their voices rose above the noise of the train and filled the entire car.

The man's head and upper body didn't show the slightest movement. He slowly let his eyelids droop and, like a child fighting against drowsiness who finally gives in, he closed his eyes. J saw how his skin, and the wrinkles the color of dead leaves around his closed eyelids, gradually turned the color of roses. Now he resembled the drunken, vacuous wild boar on the Gordon's Gin label. Suddenly J realized that the entire group of schoolgirls had stopped talking. Only the noise of the train could still be heard. The schoolgirls' expressions were ugly and afraid. They were young girls now, with rough underdeveloped faces, frozen by fear. Only the man with his eyes closed looked happy as he stood there, enraptured, with that rosy glow. J was stricken with fear, as if he himself were in danger. One more minute, and the girls would begin to cry and scream. The stranger would be arrested for indecency.

Just then the train stopped in Nippori, and the doors opened. J jumped up and pushed his way through the schoolgirls until he was in front of the *chikan*. He seized the arm of his camel overcoat, and dragged him by force out onto the platform. The doors closed behind them as soon as they were out of the train. J looked back at the schoolgirls who were glaring at him and the old man from the other side of the glass. The smallest girl in the group, J could see, was blushing crimson red and seemed ready to burst into tears. The old man had probably touched her breasts or something as he surrendered to his solitary sexual rapture. . . .

"You were a little too careless," J apologized as he released his arms from the old man's chest. By this time, he was becoming upset and even felt some self-disgust.

"Thank you. If you hadn't been so kind as to help me, I'm afraid I might've gone all the way," the old man said frankly.

That was how J and the old man became "street friends" and went on to the bar in Unebi-machi to have a drink together.

The young man joined J and the old man, and they began to meet regularly at the bar in Unebi-machi before setting out into the crowds of the city. After graduating from high school, the boy hadn't gone on to college or looked for a job. Instead, he had focused all of his passion on writing a stormy poem on perversion. Neither J nor the old man tried to make the boy talk about himself in more detail than that. There was no need for it. They didn't even know each others' names. But almost every day, from morning until evening, sometimes even through the night, the three of them were together, riding subways, loitering on trains and streetcars, on jolting bus trips from Shinbashi to Shibuya. They were a harmoniously matched group. To each other, they were the most loyal of "street friends."

Everything the boy wore was of the highest quality, from his English trench coat (somewhat out of season in mid-winter) to his suits, shirts, ties, and shoes—all somewhat extravagant for his age. But there were many days when he had only a few coins in his pockets, and sometimes the old man and J would slip money into his trench coat. It didn't bother him at all and he never refused. He would spend all the money they gave him the same day, on things like garishly decorated leather ski gloves. If he touched a girl's backside with those gloves, she would suspect nothing. Instead, she would imagine that a miniature military tank was running down her flank, they were such completely impractical, ornate gloves.

J, the old man, and the boy went out into the crowds together but, since the boy had joined them, only the old man acted as a pervert while J and the boy devoted themselves entirely to security duties. The boy had made it clear from the start that his intentions were limited to that role, and J unexpectedly found himself standing next to the boy. The old man carried on as before, acting like a veteran *chikan* and showed no interest in the change in J. His zeal bordered on the fanatical and, like J before him, the boy seemed willing to bow before the superiority of the older *chikan*.

As they watched over the old man's activities from another

corner of the car, J and the boy sometimes discussed what it meant to be a *chikan*. The boy thought incessantly about his poem in praise of sexual deviance, and whenever the conversation turned to the topic, he would become obsessive and talk at length, regardless of their surroundings. The boy, on principle, could not accept deviants who took precautionary measures against danger. He confessed that he had come to feel an awe for the old man, but he, too, had something of the fanatic about him. It was difficult for him to find anything admirable in safety and he consistently rejected anything that muddied the image of the fearless *chikan*, the hero of his poem.

"You yourself," the boy would say, "you barely get excited by these deviant acts which don't involve any risk in places where there's no danger at all. Isn't it only because this mutual aid between *chikans* isn't one hundred percent safe that you can feel some excitement, no matter how small? There's no such thing as perfect safety. A *chikan* is just like a big-game hunter. Most hunters would be bored in a great savanna where the lions and rhinos come purring up to them meek as kittens. A hunter would become neurotic in a place like that!"

J never lost interest in these discussions with the teenager, probably because they forced him to think about his own decision to become a *chikan*.

"Doesn't the idea of a safe *chikan* bother you?" the boy repeated.

"You're right, it does. But if it really is the destiny of the deviant to be caught and to experience the ultimate humiliation and taste the greatest danger, there's no need to hurry it, is there? It's the same as death. We're all going to die sooner or later, so what's the point in rushing it?"

"No, it's a mistake to put it that way. If death were the only thing that revealed the meaning of life, I'd want to die as soon as I could. If running the risk of being arrested is one of the intrinsic characteristics of the deviant, then whoever excludes that element can't be a true deviant. He's a fake. In the end he's nothing at all. He'll get bored and fed up with it. The hero of my poem isn't that kind of contemptible character. But what I don't understand is how the old man can be so completely alone when the two of us are here to protect him. It's almost more than I can stand to watch. He looks like a real *chikan* in real danger," the boy said, watching the old man, who was lost in his own world in the crowded bus, with his eyes closed. His eyelids had already taken on that rosy coloring.

J confided to the boy that he suspected the old man had a nest of cancer lodged in his strong body or that he was deeply worried about his heart symptoms. After that, the boy became more devoted to the old man. Perhaps he was considering giving the dying *chikan* a supporting role in his poem.

The boy often discussed with J his plans for his next decisive deviant action. These plans frightened J. They were clearly criminal, and once the boy had enacted one of them, there would be no way for J and the old man to help him. His plans went beyond the realm of perversity and into that of brutal, sex crime.

"Forget it. Even if you think only of yourself, you can't do such things. If you do, you'll be forced out of society before you can write your poem. Why do you have to carry things so far to write your poem?"

"If you think about it, it might be something I have to do, not for the poem, but so that I can become my true self," the boy said mysteriously.

J didn't really believe the teenager's daydreams, but he had gradually developed a deep feeling of friendship for the boy, and he wanted to try to free him from his fantasies. Perhaps something else was at work in J's mind: J knew that, as a deviant himself, he risked becoming a dangerously spined sea urchin like the boy and that frightened him. So in removing the boy's spines, he was in fact hoping to protect himself. . . .

Late one night, when J and the old man were alone in the hotel bar in Unebi-machi, J made a suggestion.

"I think I'll take the boy to see a girl I've known for a while, a kind of semi-prostitute. It might be better for him if we could shift his poetic interest away from perverted heroes to more lyrical poems about sensual love."

"You should try. If he wants to become a *chikan*, he's still got plenty of time to change—he can do it at sixty," the old man laughed.

So J called his friend and took the boy to her place. He explained the situation and persuaded her that the boy should experience a completely normal sexual relationship at least once. The boy smiled vaguely as he listened to J's pleading. He asked J to wait in the hotel bar because he felt a little nervous. The boy's words seemed to flatter the woman. But it was the woman who called J on the phone, practically in tears as she screamed, "Come and get this monster out of here!" J had barely finished his first glass of Pernod. By the time he got to the room, the boy was sitting serenely on a chair, with his tie carefully knotted, smiling the way he always did. The woman was in the shower, making frantic, violent sounds as if out of her mind. J looked into the bathroom to say he was taking the boy with him. When she turned to look at him, she was ghostly pale, perhaps (or perhaps not) because of the icy shower. "I'm finished with you, too," she screamed at J. As J closed the door, he noticed some drops of blood on the tiles beside the bathtub. The boy didn't say anything, and J didn't question him. He had done something terrible.

From then on, neither J nor the old man made any special attempt to intervene in the boy's affairs. The three calmly resumed their "street friends" habit of cruising the city, but they knew that, ultimately, the boy was not there to stay. He was merely resting, sheltered by J and the old man, before embarking on his second major deviant act. He was a traveler taking a brief respite.

Winter was coming to an end. At night, thunder rolled through the sky and intermittent rain poured down. In early morning, the sun spread its warmth, still tepid as a cat's belly. J's wife made a schedule of outdoor locations with the cameraman and pasted it to the wall of the work space. They would probably be shooting her new film from spring through early summer. One morning J met the old man and the two of them went to the bar in Unebi-machi. For several days, the boy had stayed away from them. He seemed to have fallen into a depression. And by now, when the boy wasn't around, both J and the old man felt their excitement was at a lower level when they entered the crowd. So, that morning, neither of them could resist a warm smile when they discovered the boy waiting for them at the hotel bar in Unebi-machi. J remembered—though only vaguely—how the old man's face used to fill with such pleasure that it was nearly ugly when he caught sight of J in the days when they were still only two. And just as J had been then, the boy was clearly in a bad mood, as if he disliked both of them. He placed a bottle of sleeping pills and a tumbler of whisky on the low table in front of his chair. They said nothing about the fact that he was mixing liquor and pills so early in the morning, but they couldn't watch his behavior with indifference. They tried to relax and smile as they shifted in their chairs, in silence, facing the boy.

"I've finished my second period of preparation," the boy said. "I'm going to do it."

The old man and J looked at him. Their smiling cheeks and lips stiffened. The boy's face was flushed with warmth by the sleeping pills and whisky. He had a cunning expression that vividly reminded the old man and J of the night they had met him, desperate, wearing only boots and a trench coat over his naked body. His eyes were bloodshot and seemed to bulge, and his face was deadly pale and dirty. His voice quavered hysterically, the hoarse voice of an angry child.

"But you're wearing a suit today. And you even have your pants on, haven't you? Are you going to lock yourself up in a restroom somewhere and change into your lightweight uniform?" the old man said to the boy. His awkwardly derisive tone seemed as if it were meant to hide his uneasiness.

"No, I won't do the same thing as before. Didn't I tell you so the first time when you got in my way?" the boy said. When he said "got in my way" instead of "rescued me," J felt as if the boy were spitting on his friendship.

"You aren't seriously going to carry out one of the crazy fantasies you told me about—raping someone on the train or stabbing an old woman to death on the subway," J said, trying to stay calm.

"I'm not telling anyone about my plans. The minute I do, they will vanish into thin air like a mirage. Anyway, can't you just leave me alone now? All I promised when I joined you was to be the special lifeguard for this *chikan* club. So from now on, just leave me alone!" the boy said.

"If that's the case, why did you go to so much trouble to tell us you've finished your preparations and you're ready for your second big adventure? Shouldn't you have kept quiet and gone off somewhere to carry it out alone?"

"I only came to say goodbye," the boy said. "After all, aren't we friends?" He was so frank and honest that it moved J and the old man. Then his radiant, bloodshot eyes clouded with tears, and he stood up roughly, like a violent child. "Don't get in my way. It nearly killed me, the pain and suffering it took to make up my mind to go through with it this time. I've made my sacrifices, and I've made up my mind, so I want you to get out of my way. I really can't stand you safe deviants, in it for half the fun. If you try to stop me, I'll go to the police and tell them what a pair of *chikan* you two really are!"

The boy left the hotel at a run. The old man and J paid the bill and followed him. The sidewalk was dry and no longer showed any trace of snow. J and the old man were breathing hard as they tailed the boy, who was taking long strides, as if driven by anger. He was heading toward the National Railways Unebi-machi Station. Suddenly he turned his head slyly. When he saw J and the old man, he made a gesture to show that his annoyance was getting the better of him. He stood motionless and continued to glare at them. J and the old man approached him hesitantly.

"Why are you following me?" the boy shouted. He had lost his equilibrium under the repeated assault of sleeping pills and whisky. He was no longer his normal self. His sturdy upper body was slowly tilting to one side, then suddenly became erect, and then began to lean again.

"It's gone to your head. Go home and sleep. We'll take you there by taxi."

"Why are you following me? Don't you know this is none of your business? This is important to me!" The boy was screaming and waving his arms as if to threaten them. They were in a busy shopping street, and people began to gather immediately.

"Okay, we won't interfere. But you can't stop us from watching your adventure, can you? We want to be there when you become a real *chikan*. I mean, I can't imagine you're going to have the freedom to write your poem after you go through with this adventure. So go on and do what you have to do. Don't worry about us rescuing you or getting in your way. If you're afraid now, I guess it must be real fear you're feeling," J said. He had gradually become more and more irritated, and in the end he'd spoken with hatred.

For just an instant, a meek, surprised expression returned to the boy's face, and he stared at J. Then suddenly he turned and began to walk away. He didn't look back again, and was absorbed in himself, as if he'd already completely forgotten them. They followed him at a distance of about a hundred feet, without speaking.

The boy went into the Unebi-machi Station. After he'd passed through the gate, J and the old man went to the ticket window. They bought their tickets without hurrying and by the time they passed through the gate, the boy had already begun to work. He was standing next to a vendor's booth sandwiched between two sets of stairs that diverged in a fan shape toward the platforms for Kanda and Ikebukuro. In his right hand, he held the hand of a little girl. With his left hand, he was holding up a toy for her to see. It was a red battery-powered monkey. He leaned forward a little and said something to the girl. Then he gave her the toy monkey and, side by side, the two of them climbed the stairs to the platform on the Kanda-bound side. They gave an impression of shared, secret intimacy, as if they were brother and sister, which made the people who watched them smile. Only J and the old man did not smile. They realized that the boy intended to kidnap the girl, but they were struck dumb by the fear that this realization aroused.

When the teenager and the child had reached the top of the stairs and disappeared from sight, the door of the bathroom behind the vendor's booth was pushed open and a young woman came out. She looked around and called out to someone in a low timid voice. Then, as if prompted by fear, she started up the stairs toward the Ikebukuro platform, crying out the child's name. She seemed about to fall several times, but she climbed the stairs with agility. At the same time, the old man and J took one step forward. They wanted to shout to the woman, to warn her to take the other stairs. But they both remained silent. Their lips were tightly closed, and their hands dangled uselessly. Could they be still under the spell of the teenager's words?

A second later, the woman's cry of protest descended on them like a plummeting kite. J didn't have time to look back at the old man. He ran up the stairs the boy and the little girl had climbed, taking several steps at a time. He arrived at an excruciating, pathetic scene. A Yamanote Line train was rumbling in along the platform. On the opposite platform, the young woman was stretching out her arms, about to dive onto the tracks. The little girl who was clutching the red monkey was struggling in the ditch of iron-colored gravel between the tracks. The boy was on his knees on the track where the train was approaching. Throwing the girl into the safe ditch, he had twisted the top half of his body upward like a fallen horse. His arms were now empty and he seemed about to neigh at the sky. He folded them tightly against his chest. Just before J closed his eyes, he saw something that was like a strange, wondrous vision: the front of the train was suddenly dyed crimson red with the boy's blood.

J screamed and started to cry.

An hour later, J and the old man were sitting shoulder to shoul-der on a couch in the hotel bar in Unebi-machi. In silence, each of them stared at the other's trembling glass. J recalled the words of the sobbing young woman as she appealed over and over to the crowd that had gathered around her. "That man was a god," she said, holding the little girl to her chest. "My little girl saw me and jumped from the platform down onto the tracks. Everybody could see she was going to be killed! I could see it too. But that man, like a god he was, he saved her, and then the poor thing . . ."

"When all's said and done, that boy was simply trying to live his life as a *chikan*. If I think of that, it gives me a miserable bit of peace of mind," the old man said. "But a *chikan*, even if he risks his life as that boy did, cannot but continue to be a *chikan*. He was a danger-ous man. A club of safe deviants like us, is in my opinion simply a way of diluting the poison."

"The boy said the same thing to me more than once," J said.

"In the end, there's something fraudulent about us. I've realized that we either have to become dangerous deviants who take risks like him, or we have to give it up altogether. Those are the only two possible roads," the old man said.

"I feel the same way. I'll probably never come to this bar after today, and I doubt I'll have the honor of meeting you again," J said with deep sorrow.

"You'll probably stop being a *chikan*. And I'll become a more dangerous one, I suppose. I've had this presentiment that someday I'll be arrested in a crowd on the subway and die of a heart attack."

J stood up. The old man remained seated, looked up at J, and shook his head. He blushed around his eyes and smiled sadly—like the drunken wild boar on the Gordon's Gin label—as he did when he was burning with anger or sexually aroused. A mist of white tears covered his predatory eyes. They were the gentlest eyes the old man had ever shown to J. J was moved to tears again. Like the old man, he smiled slightly, shook his head, and remained silent. He left the bar and the hotel. He was lightheaded and afraid that he might col-lapse while the old man was watching him. In the taxi the bellboy found for him, J was utterly desperate and choked with tears. He'd just lost the two best friends he'd ever had.

J spent the next couple of weeks holed up in his apartment. During that time, he realized that it was a burden and a source of pain for his wife that he never went out of the house any more. And not only for his wife. The cameraman, who was coming regularly to the work space to do preproduction work on the film, showed the same reaction to J's presence. But since J was thinking about nothing but the boy and the old man, he didn't pursue the deeper meaning of these reactions. He was as uncomprehending as an infant.

His own feelings were such that even when the cameraman finally came into his bedroom late one morning and solemnly said there was something he wanted to talk about, J still thought it must have to do with the film's production costs or the need to use the Jaguar. But the cameraman confessed that he had fallen in love with J's wife and, as a result, she was pregnant. J stared in disbelief at the middle-aged man with his ridiculous mustache planted on a face that was big and round and black as a whale's, staring at him with bloodshot eyes. It seemed perfectly natural to J that he experienced no particularly cruel feelings of pain. How on earth could this be? How could something like this possibly happen between this outsider, a middle-aged man who loved precision instruments, and J's wife, with her meager, boyish body, who was only interested in making films? J found it hard to believe. And could his wife, with her unfeminine hips, really be capable of pregnancy? She'd probably die during childbirth.

"I know it must be a shock to you to be betrayed by your oldest friend, J," the cameraman said, as though he was trying to comfort him. Oldest friend? J objected to that. The only beings the word "friend" truly evoked for him now were a dead teenager and a solitary old man who at this very minute was undoubtedly roaming the crowded streets.

"Well, how long has it been going on?" J asked. It was a stupid question, and he blushed at the meaninglessness of his own words. Once he found out how long they'd been betraying him, then what would he do?

But the cameraman gave him an earnest answer. "Ever since you started staying away from home, J."

"And you got her pregnant in the middle of the afternoon?" J said derisively.

The cameraman's large, round, dark face blushed copper red. He stammered and spoke in a trembling voice.

"J, you are sexually perverted. From what Mitsuko has told me, it's clear that you've been using her sexually as a substitute for a boy, as a homosexual partner. To be blunt about it, when a sexually perverted man is married, another man *should* have a sexual relationship with the wife. It's his duty."

J imagined the cameraman and his wife gossiping about his sexual proclivities, and for the first time, he was seized with a fierce anger. The cameraman seemed to be waiting for a beating which he intended to endure without resistance. In the end, J didn't resort to violence. Instead he felt the cancer of self-loathing, which had lodged itself so persistently in the recesses of his heart, beginning to dissolve.

"So what do you intend to do?" J asked with affection, while he looked into the cameraman's red, insecure eyes.

"I'll marry Mitsuko and we'll have the child, assuming you'll give her a divorce," the cameraman said excitedly.

"And what about your own wife and child?"

"I suppose I'll give them an allowance. If I can, I'd like to take care of the child myself, though."

"It's going to be tough," J said.

"Yes, it'll be tough. And we still have to finish the film," the cameraman said. His dull, fixed expression, so middle-aged, was gradually changing, beginning to glow with a proud self-confidence. J felt pity and compassion for him, but he wondered how many people would have to suffer the hardships of the real world for the sake of this man's recklessness, this man who could easily have been a tribal leader in some patriarchal society.

"I'll file the divorce papers as soon as I can," J said. "Have you already looked for somewhere to live with Mitsuko?"

"No, not yet."

"Then I'll leave. I can move in with my father for a while," J said.

"J, thank you," the bearded cameraman said. He was moved. Suddenly his shoulders began to shake as softly as a woman's, releasing all the tension from his body. He returned to the work space with childish sobs in the back of his throat.

For some time J stayed in bed, lying on his back without moving. No thoughts came to him. Occasionally he could hear his wife and the cameraman whispering in the work space. Then he packed his clothes and personal belongings in a suitcase, went down the kitchen stairs to the garage without speaking to his wife, and, for the first time in months, got into the Jaguar. J drove to the headquarters of a steel company in Marunouchi to visit his father, who was president of the company. He told his father about the divorce and asked him to understand what had happened and why he would be moving back into his father's house that same day. J's father smiled gently as he heard J out. Then he asked, "How old are you?"

"I'm thirty," J replied. The word "thirty" echoed oddly in his ears. In some strange way he felt guilty. Thirty? At this age, he was no longer a child.

"You've lived like a hermit ever since your first wife killed herself. But now your second wife has been sleeping with another man, and she's leaving you. Doesn't that even things up? How about it? You're thirty already, aren't you about ready to start leading a normal life again? This company is building a revolutionary mercury-alloy plant, and as part of the groundwork, I'm going on a tour of our American partners. Why don't you come along as my secretary? And why don't you take a job at the new plant? I'll show you some slides of a forty-story building that was built with nothing but this alloy. It'll excite you. It's something worth doing. I know you're going to take me up on my offer and start a new life for yourself!"

J thought about the offer as he sat watching the slide show with his father. Now that his old friends and wife had left him, one new friend had died in an accident, and the other had vanished into the crowd of ten million people in Tokyo, he was completely alone. This was certainly a chance to return to his old conformist life. To his real life. Of course he knew that it was self-deception, even emotionally, to cancel out his sense of responsibility and guilt for his first wife's suicide with his second wife's adultery and betrayal. But wasn't the very act of acknowledging that self-deception the first step in his rehabilitation to the life of a conformist? He felt that he was beginning now to lay one self-deception on top of another and would go on doing so until he was indistinguishable from the aging monster who was sitting beside him, growling like a disgruntled animal as he watched his color slides. It felt like resignation, and at the same time it felt like being rescued after drifting at sea for too long, even if it was rescue by an enemy ship. . . .

In the end J gave in to his father and accepted the offer. His departure for America was three weeks away. His daily life would suddenly turn full circle. As he left the president's office, walked down the long corridor, and got into the elevator, he imagined his father, whom he had just left, as the image of himself forty years from now. His father now and himself in forty years, both would remain perfectly composed even if they had cancer or faced the risk of heart attack. Neither would ever lose the poker face of conformism. Yes, his new life as a self-deceiving conformist had just begun. Swinging his shoulders vigorously like a busy, capable, company man, he exited through the automatic door of the building and headed toward his Jaguar, which was parked next to the subway entrance. Suddenly he was so excited he thought he would faint. Abandoning the Jaguar, he ran, nearly jumped, down the stairs into the subway.

He boarded a crowded subway car and, without hesitating, advanced steadily through the tight throng of bodies. With no uncertainty, almost as if by prior arrangement, he arrived at a spot behind a young woman. He took a quick look around. The sound of hot blood ringing in his ears had already swallowed up the rumbling of the train and the noise of the passengers' voices. He closed his eyes tightly and rubbed his naked penis repeatedly in the warm intimacy of the girl's buttocks. They were as fat as a pheasant's and they offered him resistance. At once he saw himself as someone who was taking a step forward with no possibility of retreat. A new life, a new life with no deception. With low moans sounding in his blazing head, he climaxed.

The rest of the world sprang to life again. Surely and ineradicably staining the woman's coat, his semen was real, a piece of evidence. The ten million strangers of Tokyo glared at J with hostile eyes. *J!* they seemed to call. Fear struggled against bliss in a wave that rose up interminably and engulfed him. Countless arms had seized him. Overcome with fear, J began to cry. He considered his tears to be his compensation for those his wife had cried the night she killed herself.

(1963)

Translated from the Japanese by Luk Van Haute

Sarcophagus and Maracas

—August 10, 1962, Summer sesshin,
Joei Temple, service for Koetsu

Fat, he was the butt of jokes,
farting his sake smell in zazen, chanting for alms
in sleep. Now his bed's rolled up
like a rare shell, begging bowl inside.

The sarcophagus is slanted upward,
as if traveling at great speed.
"Plenty of solid fuel for this zen rocket!"
he'd blurt out while chiseling, making us howl.
How could he keep forgetting, we marveled,
that he'd said it before?

Filing by, we now read his last waka, set
deeply in the granite hood:

Why waver over meanings?
Moon silvering all,
absorb the tracks of birds
on this spit of sand.

Sotatsu's egrets, brittle, hung for the occasion,
soar in emptiness above . . .

So in this newspaper photo they too
seem to want to make us laugh:
Four mariachis at Peace Park,
open-mouthed and looking skyward,
shaking their maracas . . .*

Untitled

—dedicated to Origuchi[†]

Her kisses tasted of blood, or wellwater flecked with rust?

She folded her Rose of the Snow kimono over the corner of
the futon.

So you think she knew your suffering in advance?

Not knew, but represented it.

What do you mean, the right to private violence?

In her company the world was no more than the splashing water
of her voice.

---

* Yasusada was a lay zennist and became a resident student for a brief period
during the early 1960s. Sotatsu was a zen priest and painter of the late sixteenth
and early seventeenth centuries. Peace Park is built on the flashpoint site of the
atomic bomb. Apparently entered at a later date, the last stanza in the original
is written in a different colored ink than the rest of the poem.

† Origuchi Shinobu, novelist and critic. Both editions of Origuchi's masterpiece,
Shisha no sho (*Book of the Dead*), published under the pseudonym Shaku Choku,
were found, heavily annotated, amongst Yasusada's belongings.

Do you rise like the sun over an automobile graveyard?

I wake from dreams worn out and dull as a horse.

Did you free yourself from the obligations of fidelity?

Her clinging dress always made me shiver.

What did she show you that you had not already seen?

The swing phase of her walk was highly derived.

You bet on a ghost, knowing you would lose?

On the upstroke, her clavicles folded in like a jackknife.

If not in clear, distinct ideas, in what did you believe?

We were hurtling through a transparent mirror.

What did she see in the fullness of your lips?

The heartshaped impression of her clitoris.

6

You turn on and off, and

If I pass my tongue through your speaking mouth, I know that there
       is nothing there. But if I hold my tongue inside a written
       sentence,

It blisters.

This is an act of forgetting that the dead are dead and that is
       that. Forgetting the candle held behind the figure speaking

Behind the screen.

Or does the mouth, calligraphic friend, cast its own shadows?
       "At Hiroshima," you write, "the shadows of the victors were
       as if photographed into concrete building blocks."

Or are they just turned on for a long time? Or do we two share
                            a forgotten tongue?

Or do they funnel us both to the ideograph barely legible on the
                                     paper

       screen—

The space around it

Where the shadow and the mouth are one?*

Translated from the Japanese by Tosa Motokiyu,
Ojiu Norinaga, and Okura Kyojin

---

*This poem is a transformation of poem #6 in Jack Spicer's 1965 collection
Language. The direct quote from Spicer's original has been altered: Yasusada
has changed "victims" to "victors."

The Chess Players

N o tricks, I'm warning you," growled my opponent from the other side of the board, where he was adjusting the position of his useless glasses on his nose. "Move the pieces as God commands. I won't be able to see if your moves are fair, but I'll find out sooner or later—my sense of touch is amazing."

Casually I told him that I, too, was nearsighted, perhaps even a little more so than he, and that, as much as I tried, I could see neither the board nor the position of the pieces clearly, but that through practice, my sense of touch had also become remarkable.

"So, you'd better play fair, too," I warned, "or I assure you there'll be hell to pay."

Thus we initiated that strange game of chess, without spectators, and for a while everything went smoothly. I remember quite well that I was white. I advanced my king's pawn, and he advanced his, understanding that what I intended was to dominate the center of the board. Then I moved the knight on the right and my rival moved the knight on his right, which, obviously, was on my left. To be sure that we were moving the pieces we really wished to move, we stroked them beforehand with the tips of our forefingers, determining their shapes.

In the beginning, we played fairly. After a dozen moves, however, the irregularities began.

"Check, with my bishop," he threatened unexpectedly, after a brief and peremptory snort.

"Which bishop are you referring to?" I asked.

"You will find it right behind your king. Two squares further," he replied.

"That is not possible, sir," I protested, passing my finger over his so-called bishop. "This piece is a pawn." Then I warned him: "Get your queen out of there or I'll take her with my knight."

"Not a chance," he said. "Neither of your knights, jump as they may, can reach my queen. She's too far away. Don't get clever."

"In that case," I insisted, "I'll take your bishop with this castle. I don't think I can let you go."

"With what castle?" he exclaimed, recognizing by touch the shape of the pawn I had intended to pass for a castle. "Where has this castle put its battlements? Do you really think I'm a fool?"

"All right," I told him, "let's drop this absurd game. Let's forget it. You know as well as I that it was only an excuse to determine which of us is more of a scoundrel. If what you want now is to see which of us is stronger, let's go out to the street. There we'll really be able to have it out and we'll see who cries victory."

We felt along the wall for the front door, but the bartender blocked our way.

"Let's have the party in peace," he said. "No fights. I don't want the customers fighting in the doorway of my establishment. I don't want disturbances in the neighborhood. It would be much better for you to sit back down and go on playing."

We had no choice but to remain on opposite sides of the table, separated by the board. We went on taking each other's pieces, without worrying about fairness, and we ended up each with our respective kings.

"Draw," I whispered.

"Draw," he accepted.

For a long while, neither of us spoke, and we did not move our gaze from the board, as though we were truly eager to know which squares our kings had landed on after the battle. Five minutes later, we had become two men who no longer needed to hide their impotence and who, instead of getting irritated over nothing, accepted their limits with resignation. I told him my name was Juan and that I was a watchmaker, but for the past eight years, I had been stone broke due to a serious diabetic affliction that had left me practically blind. He then told me that his name was Rafael, and that, until they had operated on him unsuccessfully for cataracts, he had worked as a guard at the Regional Agronomic Institute. He confessed, as well, that he was a widower and childless, and I said that, there at least, I was ahead of him, because I was a bachelor and not tormented by the memory of a gentle wife who had passed away. I told him that happily, with a smile, and he didn't take it the wrong way.

"Do you think, Rafael, my friend," I asked him at last, "that once we were men with eyes that could see everything?"

"I think so," he murmured, on the point of tears. "I think we were, but the truth is I can hardly remember how things were then."

The New Inquisitors

At the end of last year, as an official representative of the town of K., I attended a sparkling reception that took place in the castle of J. at the close of the Second National Congress on Medieval Heraldry. Strategically, I took up position in front of the table, where a varied and copious spread of hors d'oeuvres was available, and from there, ignored by all the learned personages, I prepared to watch the course of events.

I noticed right away that all the guests (no fewer than a hundred, some accompanied by their wives) were heavy smokers. They lit one cigarette after another and the smoke rose slowly to the magnificent, coffered ceiling, rebounded, and came back down toward the smokers, wrapping us all in a dense fog that made us practically invisible. The rock crystal ashtrays on the tables, however, shone pristinely without a single cigarette butt in them. The air was so thick you could have cut it with a knife, but none of the servants (there were several discreetly stationed beside the door to the salon, observing the guests with vulture eyes) ventured to open the windows. I imagined that they had received orders to resist at all costs, and they were determined to meet that goal, cost what it may.

So I continued my vigil beside the hors d'oeuvres table, receiving the nudges and confused smiles of all those who came in search of croquettes and fried prawns, not far from the spot where Count W. (owner of the castle and Honorary President of the Association of

Medievalists) was conversing with a group of people.

"I must confess," he was saying in a pompous tone, "that since my college days, I've felt a profound respect for Descartes. He sought the truth within himself and was the first to warn that even to *think* that everything is false, we must first *be* something."

"Cogito ergo sum," recalled someone near him.

"I smoke, therefore I am," he joked in turn.

And through the thick curtain of smoke, I thought I saw the wide and elegant movement of his left hand taking the cigarette from his mouth and throwing it to the ground. I saw, also, how he immediately brought another to his lips and how, through the fog, sparks shone from various lighters.

"Well, I think," someone was saying in another group nearby, "the principal characteristic of Chinese glazed pottery is precisely the fact that it aspired to an academic language."

His cigarette butt dropped between his feet in a rain of cinders that was half put out by the sole of a patent leather shoe.

"The worst of all," declared a high pitched voice behind me, "is the right's obsession with starting a special investigation of arms sales to the Middle East."

"And what do you say of that insane desire on the left to legalize abortion—and, worse, to make it free?"

"Look," suggested another voice, "forget the right or the left. Like the man said, below the belt we're all liberals."

"That's true," an old man with a tremulous voice agreed almost immediately. "Why must we pay the cost of abortions that we, unfortunately, are no longer able to necessitate?"

It didn't cease to surprise me that all these brilliant investigators of the past, instead of talking about bars, quarters, and fleurs-de-lys, were discussing such modern themes and, moreover, that they should seem so frivolous about a question as serious as abortion. The old man's intervention had provoked a chorus of guffaws, and that laughter served as an excuse for everyone around him, in a synchronized movement that seemed almost rehearsed, to throw their respective cigarette butts to the ground.

We had been in that salon for more than half an hour (the first guests had arrived at seven o'clock sharp), and the floor, splendidly carpeted, was already covered with hundreds of half-smoked cigarettes, many of them still burning.

"There's no doubt," someone to my left assured his companions, as he made his way through to the food, "that the best way to solve the problems of urban transportation lies in the decentralization of places of business—the effect being that a considerable number of suburban residents could carry out their activities without leaving their own communities."

Again I was impressed that one of those dusty researchers, whom I had always imagined oblivious to the issues of their time, might even have an idea for solving the city's transportation problems. Meanwhile, other smoking cigarette butts were falling to the ground and one of them, launched perhaps with excessive joy, must have fallen into the generous décolletage of the woman to my right. It slid burning down the milky way of her chest, causing a prolonged shriek which, however, did not seem to worry the gentlemen around her.

"Why do you think they are doing it?" I finally asked my colleague Diodoro H., representative from the town of A., which bordered on my own. "Why are they behaving like this?"

"Don't you see?" Diodoro whispered in my ear. "What these gentlemen are looking to do is start a fire. That's really all that matters to them. What they want, believe me, is to perish in the flames and die purified."

"Then you think they are nostalgic for the Inquisition?"

"Not the slightest doubt," Diodoro replied. "These men, and the ladies accompanying them, want to become the inquisitors of their own sins."

"Still," I objected, "they seem happy and cheerful. I've even heard them tell each other jokes."

"Don't trust appearances. They do it to throw you off track. They're trying to deceive you and deceive themselves right up to the end. I'll tell you again, the only thing that really interests them is to die in the flames. I'm sure that were they properly psychoanalyzed, obscure guilt complexes would come to light."

"But what can be tormenting them to the point of desiring such a horrible death?" I asked, my skin covered with goosebumps.

"I don't know," answered Diodoro. "Maybe it's the consciousness of their myopia. Notice that they are all, without exception, nearsighted. They have ruined their eyes reading ancient documents. They've reached the conclusion, perhaps, that their sacrifice has been futile, and that, in these times, nearsighted people like them are relics that the world can do without. It may even be that they've been wait-ing for this Congress in order to transform the castle into an immense funeral pyre."

At last the fire broke out. One of the cigarettes hit the curtains and in an instant the salon was in flames. The servants (likely under orders from Count W.) rushed around, disconnecting the telephones in the salon so that, once the hour of truth arrived, no one might be tempted to notify the fire department. Faithful to the final hour, those servants died with their masters, but Diodoro and I were able to escape the inferno before the doors were closed for good.

Translated from the Spanish by Jason Weiss

Concept Tableaux

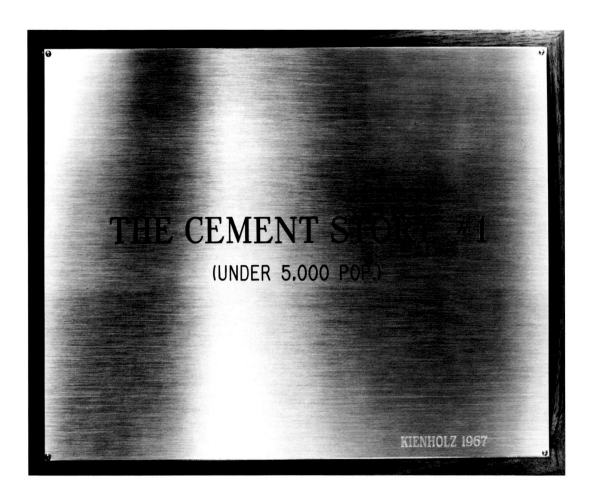

THE CEMENT S[TORE] #1

(UNDER 5,000 POP.)

KIENHOLZ 1967

THE CEMENT STORE #1
(under 5,000 pop.)

This tableau will be made from an existing grocery store in a town
anywhere in the United States with a population under 5,000. The
building must be made of either cinder blocks, cement blocks, adobe
bricks or form poured concrete. The building, businesses and inven-
tory must be purchased and left intact. The windows will be replaced
by clear plexiglass or bullet proof glass to withstand internal pressures
and resist malicious breaking. The doorway will be board formed in
such a way to allow the door to swing both ways. A section of roof
will be removed and the interior of the store will be filled with concrete completely covering all merchandise, cash register, records,
etc. The roof section will then be replaced and repaired. The board
forms at doorway will be removed, the hardened concrete now making
it impossible to enter the building. The store will be left with little
or no explanation other than it is now some sort of an art object and
no longer subject to improved property taxes.

PRICE: Part One $15,000

                              Part Two $1,000

                              Part Three   Cost plus artist's wages

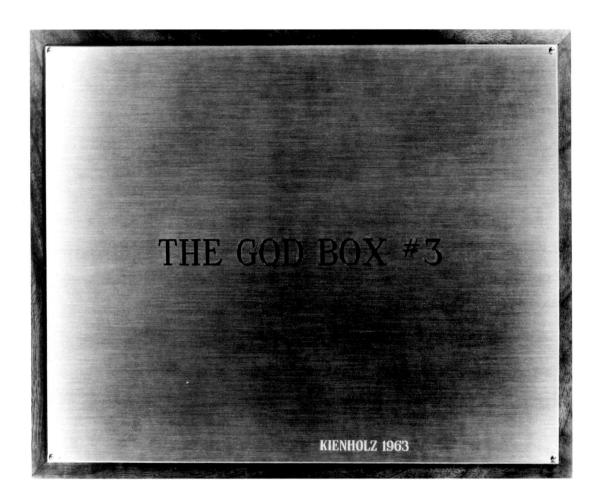

THE GOD BOX #3

KIENHOLZ 1963

THE GOD BOX #3   1963

This tableau is a box numbered three in a series of boxes in size somewhere between Reich's Orgone Accumulators and a Western outhouse. The sole purpose is to stimulate thoughts on organized religions and what they have done to and for civilization.

These boxes will be made for occupancy by one person at a time. They may contain sound, could be locked from the inside, might have a lid like a coffin, etc. I choose not to describe them in exact detail.

The name "God Box" comes from a slang phrase referring to the pipe organ in radio soap operas of the 1940's.

PRICE: Part One $ 8,000.00

                Part Two   ` $ 500.00

                Part Three   Costs plus artist's wages

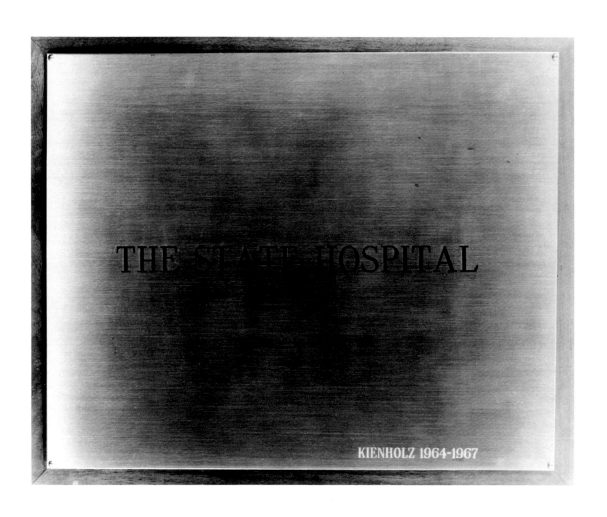

THE STATE HOSPITAL

KIENHOLZ 1964-1967

THE STATE HOSPITAL   1964

This is a tableau about an old man who is a patient in a state mental hospital. He
is in an arm restraint on a bed in a bare room. (The piece will have to include an
actual room consisting of walls, ceiling, floor, barred door, etc.) There will be
only a bedpan and a hospital table (just out of reach). The man is naked. He
hurts. He has been beaten on the stomach with a bar of soap wrapped in a towel
(to hide tell-tale bruises). His head is a lighted fish bowl with water that contains
two live black fish. He lies very still on his side. There is no sound in the room.

Above the old man in the bed is his exact duplicate, including the bed (beds will be
stacked like bunks). The upper figure will also have the fish bowl head, two black
fish, etc. But, additionally, it will be encased in some kind of lucite or plastic
bubble (perhaps similar to a cartoon balloon), representing the old man's thoughts.

His mind can't think for him past the present moment. He is committed there for
the rest of his life.

PRICE: Part One $ 15,000.00

                Part Two $ 1,000.00

                Part Three   Costs plus artist's wages

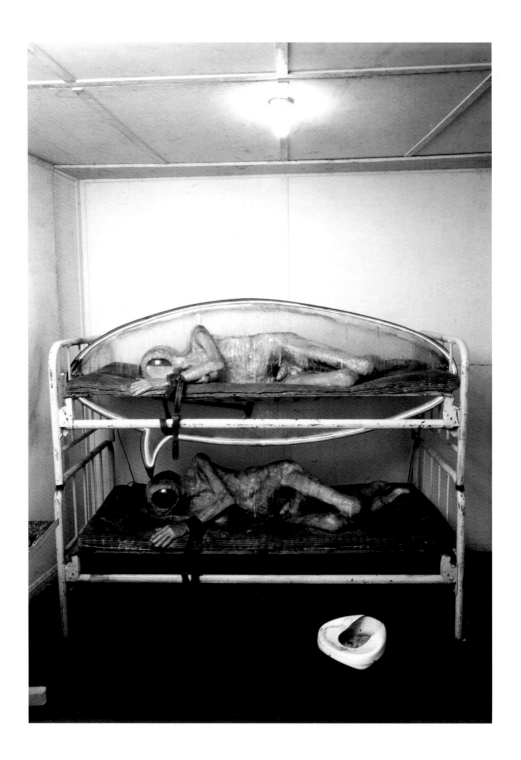

Sometime in the late 1960s, Edward Kienholz purchased a Tiffany-style glass lamp on the East Coast, which he packed very carefully for his flight back to Los Angeles. The TWA staff would not allow him to carry it on board so he warned the baggage crew that they would need to handle it with great care. When he reached Los Angeles, he discovered that the lamp had been shattered. He was seething, but he waited a few days before driving back to the TWA terminal at the Los Angeles Airport with a clipboard, paper, and a measuring tape, and very carefully examining the lost-and-found desk in TWA's baggage claim department. Kienholz went home again and wrote up a proclamation stating exactly what his lamp was worth. Then he returned to the terminal with a fire ax, marked off a length of the desk whose materials were worth the same amount as the lamp, and proceeded to destroy it. An employee got the police to apprehend him, but TWA had the intelligence not to have him arrested, realizing that they would suffer worse publicity if the affair got into the newspapers.

Kienholz's more intimate work tended, like this action, to be conceptual—long before the term "conceptual art" was at large in the land. It was simply native to him. In the mid-'60s, he began work on a series that he called "concept tableaux": he would think of a work, boil down its description to fit onto one 8½-by-11 inch piece of paper, and then etch its title onto a standard brass plaque. He would frame both title and concept and sell them together for a third of the estimated cost of building the complete work. The person who bought them owned the concept, and the buyer could have the work made if he or she could come up with the rest of the money. Kienholz once joked that this was a practical way to record the pieces he didn't have the time, money, or resources to make.

A few of the concept tableaux were sold, more in Europe than in the United States. Only four of them were ever realized: *The State Hospital, The Commercial #2, The Portable War Memorial,* and *The Art Show. The State Hospital* was the first. Kienholz was so anxious to have it made that he broke the program and went ahead with it himself. In his early twenties, he had worked as an attendant in a mental hospital in eastern Washington State. There, he saw the horror of institutionalization firsthand. In 1966, he recreated it, constructing a naked male figure from various resins and plastics and placing it on a cot. Kienholz built a second bunk above the first and placed on it a second version of the same figure, with a large neon tube wrapped around the entire bed like a cartoon thought-bubble to show that what the man on the lower bed is imagining is an exact duplicate of himself. The message: there is no escape from this situation, even through the mind. Kienholz carved out the face of each figure and replaced it with a circular goldfish bowl, with a pair of goldfish swimming in each bowl. To see a man's mind degraded to the level of a goldfish is a chilling thought, and the piece is a cautionary tale: individually or collectively, we must not become that figure.

The Art Show, which Kienholz had conceived in 1963, was completed in 1977. This work involved the creation of the interior of a commercial art gallery—complete with a reception desk, lighting system, hanging walls, and a set of works to be exhibited there. In a curiously Duchampian gesture, the work that is shown consists of all the plans and diagrams that went into the tableau's own making. Kienholz populated the piece with a cast of characters—which included curators, artists, himself, and his children—who are viewing the show. Although these figures are lifelike and based on real people, their faces have automobile air-conditioner vents as mouths, which gives them a mechanical, surreal quality, and they can often be recognized only by their body shapes or clothes.

Relatively early in his career, Kienholz was thus able to express—and give public record to—the size and scale that his work would not be able to assume until years later.

—Walter Hopps

Chivalry

On a White Flag Group speaking commitment to the Tough Shit But You Still Can't Drink Group down in Braintree this past July, Don G., up at the podium, revealed publicly about how he was ashamed that he still as yet had no real solid understanding of a Higher Power. It's suggested in the third of the Boston AA's 12 Steps that you turn your Diseased will over to the direction and love of "God as you understand Him." It's supposed to be one of AA's major selling points that you get to choose your own God. You get to make up your own understanding of God or a Higher Power or Whom-/Whatever. But Gately, at like ten months clean, at the TSBYSCD podium in Braintree, opines that at this juncture he's so totally clueless and lost he's thinking that he'd maybe rather have the White Flag Crocodiles just grab him by the lapels and just tell him what AA God to have an understanding of, and then give him totally blunt and dogmatic orders about how to turn over his Diseased will to whatever this Higher Power is. He notes how he's observed already that some Catholics and Fundamentalists now in AA had a childhood understanding of a Stern and Punishing-type God, and Gately's heard them express incredible Gratitude that AA let them at long last let go and change over to an understanding of a Loving, Forgiving, Nurturing-type God. But at least these folks started out with *some* idea of Him/Her/It, whether fucked up or no. You might think it'd be easier if you came in with 0 in the way of denominational background or preconceptions, you might think it'd be easier to sort of invent a Higher-Powerish God from scratch and then like erect an understanding, but Don Gately complains that this has not been his experience thus far. His sole experience so far is that he takes one of AA's very rare specific suggestions and hits the knees in the AM and asks for Help and then hits the knees again at bedtime and says Thank You, whether he believes he's talking to Anything/-body or not, and he somehow gets through that day clean. This, after ten months of ear-smoking concentration and reflection, is still all he feels like he "understands" about the "God angle." Publicly, in front of a very tough and hard-ass–looking AA crowd, he sort of simultaneously confesses and complains that he sort of feels like a rat that's learned one route in the maze to the cheese and travels that route in a ratty-type fashion and whatnot. W/ the God thing being the cheese in the metaphor. Gately still feels like he has no access to the Big Spiritual Picture. He feels about the ritualistic daily *Please* and *Thank You* prayers rather like a hitter who's on a hitting streak and doesn't change his jock or socks or pre-game routine for as long as he's on the streak. W/ sobriety being the hitting streak and whatnot, he explains. The whole church basement is literally blue with smoke. Gately says he feels like this is a pretty limp and lame understanding of a Higher Power: a cheese-easement or unwashed athletic supporter. He says but when he tries to go beyond the very basic rote automatic get-me-through-this-day-please stuff, when he kneels at other times and prays or meditates or tries to achieve a Big-Picture understanding of a God as he can understand Him, he feels nothing—not nothing but *Nothing*, an edgeless blankness that somehow feels worse than the sort of unconsidered atheism he Came In with. He says he doesn't know if any of this is coming through or making any sense or if it's all just still symptomatic of a thoroughgoingly Diseased will and quote "spirit." He finds himself telling the Tough Shit But You Still Can't Drink audience dark doubtful thoughts he wouldn't have fucking ever dared to tell even Ferocious Francis G., his sponsor over at the White Flag Group in Allston. He confesses publicly that at this point the God-understanding stuff kind of makes him want to puke from fear. Something you can't see or hear or touch or smell: OK; all right. But something you can't even feel? Because that's what he feels when he tries to understand something to really sincerely pray to. Nothingness. He says when he tries to pray he gets this like image in his mind's eye of the brainwaves or whatever of his prayers going out and out, with nothing to stop them, going, going, radiating out into like space and outliving him and still going and never hitting Anything out there, much less Something with an ear. Much much less Something with an ear that could then possibly give a rat's ass. He says he's both pissed off and ashamed to be talking about this stuff instead of how just completely good it is to just be getting through the day without ingesting a Substance, but there it is. This is what's going on. He's no closer to carrying out the suggestion of the 3rd Step than the day the P.O. drove him over to his halfway house from Peabody Holding. And he is afraid.

And now the same fucking thing happens again. The tough, chain-smoking TSBYSCD Group all stands and applauds and the men give two-finger whistles and people come up at the Raffle break to pump Gately's big hand and even sometimes try and hug on him. It seems like every time he forgets himself and publicizes how he's fucking up in sobriety Boston AA's fall all over themselves to tell him how good it was to hear him and to for God's sake Keep Coming, for them if not for himself, whatever the fuck that means.

The Tough Shit But You Still Can't Drink Group seems to be over 50% bikers and biker-chicks, meaning your standard leather vests and 10 cm bootheels, belt buckles with little spade-shaped knives that come out of a slot in the slide, tattoos that are more like murals, serious tits in cotton halters, big beards, Harleywear, wooden matches in mouth-corners and so forth. After the *Our Father*, as Gately and the other White Flag speakers are clustered smoking outside the door to the church basement, the sound of high-cc Hawgs being kick-started is enough to rattle your fillings. Gately can't even start to guess what it would be like to be a sober and drug-free biker. It's like what would be the point? He imagines these people polishing the hell out of their leather and like playing a lot of really precise pool.

This one sober biker that can't be much older than Gately and is nearly Gately's size—though with a really small head and a tapered jaw that makes him look kind of like a handsome mantis—as they're massed around the door he brings a car-length chopper up alongside Gately. Says it was good to hear him. Shakes his hand in the complex way of blacks and Harleyheads. He introduces his name as Robert F., though on the lapel of his leather vest it says BOB DEATH. A biker-chick's got her arms around his waist from behind, as is SOP. He tells

Gately it was good to hear somebody new share from the heart about his struggles with the God-component. It's weird to hear a biker use the Boston-AA word *share*, much less *component* or *heart*.

The other White Flaggers have stopped talking and are watching the two men sort of just awkwardly stand there, the biker embraced from behind and straddling his throbbing Hawg. The guy's got on leather spats and a leather vest with no shirt, and Gately notices the guy's got a jailhouse tatt of AA's weird little insignia of a triangle inside a circle on one big shoulder.

Robert F./Bob Death asks Gately if by any chance he's heard the one about the fish. White Flag's Glenn K. overhears and of course he's got to put his own fucking oar in, and he breaks in and asks them all if they've heard the one about What did the blind man say as he passed by the Quincy Market fish-stall, and without waiting he says He goes, "Evening, ladies." A couple male White Flaggers fall about, and Tamara N. slaps at the back of Glenn K.'s pointy head, but without real heat, as in like What are we going to do with this sick fuck.

Bob Death smiles coolly (South-Shore bikers are required to be extremely cool in everything they do) and manipulates his wooden match with his lip and says No, not that one about the fish. He has to assume a kind of bar-shout to clear the noise of his idling Hawg. He leans in more toward Gately and shouts that the one he was talking about was: This wise old whiskery fish swims up to three young fish and goes, "Morning, boys, how's the water?" and swims away; and the three young fish watch him swim away and look at each other and go, "What the fuck is water?" and then they also swim away. The young biker leans back and smiles at Gately and gives an affable shrug and blatts away, a haltertop's tits mashed against his back.

Gately's forehead was wrinkled in emotional pain all the way up Rte. 3 home. They were in the back of Ferocious Francis's old car. Glenn K. was trying to ask what was the difference between a bottle of 5-year-old Hennessy and a human female vagina. The old-timer Dicky N., up riding shotgun, told Glenn to try to fucking remember there was ladies present. Ferocious Francis kept moving the toothpick around in his mouth and looking at Gately in the rearview. Gately wanted to both cry and hit somebody. Glenn's cheap down jacket had the faint rank oily smell of a dishtowel. There was no smoking in the car: Ferocious Francis had a little oxygen tank he had to carry around and a little thin pale-blue plastic like tube thing that lay under his nose and was taped there and sent oxygen up his nose. All he'd ever say about the tank and the tube is that they were not his personal will but that he'd submitted to medical advice and now here he was, still sucking air and staying rabidly active with his Home Group, speaking.

Something they seem to omit to mention in Boston AA when you're new and out of your skull with desperation and ready to eliminate your map and they tell you how it'll all get better and better as you abstain and recover: they omit to mention that the way it gets better and you get better is through pain. Not around pain or in spite of it. They leave this out, talking instead about Gratitude and Release from Compulsion. There's serious pain in being sober, though, you find out, after time. Then now that you're clean and don't even much want substances and feel like you want to both cry and stomp somebody into goo with pain, these Boston AA's start in on telling you You're Right Where You're Supposed to Be and telling you to remember the pointless pain of active addiction and telling you that at least this sober pain now has a purpose. At least this pain means you're going somewhere, they say, instead of the contrast of the repetitive, pointless gerbil-wheel of addictive pain.

They neglect to tell you that after the urge to get high magically vanishes and you've been substanceless for maybe six or eight months, you'll begin to start "to get in touch" with why it was that you used substances in the first place. You'll start to feel why it was you got dependent on what was, when you get right down to it, an anesthetic. "Getting In Touch With Your Feelings" is another quilted-sampler-type cliché that ends up masking something ghastly deep and real, it turns out. It starts to turn out that the vapider the AA cliché, the sharper the canines of the real truth it covers.

Near the end of his residency at Ennet House, at like eight months clean and more or less free of any chemical compulsion, going to work at the Shattuck Shelter every AM and working the Steps and getting Active and pounding out meetings like a madman, Don Gately suddenly started to remember things he would just as soon not have. Actually *remember*'s probably not the best word. It was more like he started to sort of reexperience things that he'd barely even been there to experience, in emotional terms, in the first place. A lot of it was undramatic little shit, but still somehow painful. E.g. like when he was maybe 11 pretending to watch TV with his mother and pretending to listen to her PM nightly monologue, a litany of complaint and regret whose consonants got mushier and mushier. To the extent it's Gately's place to diagnose anybody else as an alcoholic, his Mom was pretty definitely an alcoholic. She drank Stolichnaya vodka in front of the TV. They weren't Cable Ready, for reasons of $. She drank little thin glasses with cut-up bits of carrot and pepper that she'd drop into the vodka. Her maiden name was Gately. Don's like organic father had been an Estonian immigrant, a wrought-iron worker, which is like sort of a welder with ambition. He'd broken Gately's mother's jaw and left Boston when Gately was still in his mother's stomach. Gately had no brothers or sisters. His Mom was subsequently involved with a live-in lover, a former Navy MP who used to beat her up on a regular schedule, hitting her in the vicinities between groin and breast so nothing showed. A skill he'd picked up as a brig guard and Shore Patrol. At about 8-10 Heinekens, the MP used to all of a sudden throw his *Reader's Digest* against the wall and get her down and beat her with measured blows, she'd go down on the floor of the apartment and he'd hit her in the hidden vicinity, timing the blows between her arms' little waves—Gately remembered she tried to ward off the blows with a fluttering downward motion of her arms and hands, as if she were beating out flames. Gately still hasn't ever quite gotten over to look at her in State Care in the Long-Term-Care Medicaid place. The MP's tongue was in the corner of his mouth and his little-eyed face wore a look of great concentration, as if he were taking something delicate apart or putting it together. He'd be on one knee knelt over her with his look of sober problem-solving, timing his shots, the blows abrupt and darting, her writhing and trying to kind of shoo them away. The darting blows. Out of the psychic blue, very detailed memories of these fights all of a sudden surfaced one afternoon as he was getting ready to mow the Ennet House lawn. It's like a lot of memories of his youth sank without bubbles when he quit school and then later only in sobriety bubbled back up to where he could get in touch with them. His mother used to call the MP a *bastuhd* and sometimes go *oof* when he landed one in the vicinity. She drank vodka with vegetables suspended in it, a habit she'd picked up from the missing Estonian, whose first name, Gately read on a torn and then fucked-upedly Scotch-taped paper out of her jewelry box after his mother's cirrhotic hemorrhage, was Bulat. The Medicaid Long-Term place was way the fuck out the Yirrell Beach bridge in Point Shirley, right across the water from the Airport. The former MP delivered cheese and then later worked in a chowder factory and kept weights in their Beverly house's garage and drank Heineken beer. The MP carefully logged each beer he drank in a little spiral notebook he used to monitor his intake of alcohol.

Gately's Mom's special couch for TV was nubby red chintz, and when she shifted from seated upright to lying on her side with her arm between her head and the little protective doily on the couch's armrest and held the glass tilting on the little space her breasts left at the cushion's edge, it was a sign she was going under. Gately at like 10 or 11 used to pretend to listen and watch TV on the floor but would really be dividing his attention between how close his Mom was to unconsciousness and how much Stolichnaya was left in the bottle. She would only drink Stolichnaya, which she called her Comrade in Arms and said Nothing But The Comrade Would Do. After she went under for the evening and he'd carefully taken the tilted glass out of her hand, Don'd take the bottle and mix the first couple vodkas with Diet Coke and drink a couple of those until it lost its fire, then drink The Comrade straight. This was like a routine. Then he'd put the near-empty bottle back next to her glass with its vegetables darkening in the undrunk vodka; she'd wake up on the couch in the morning with no idea she hadn't drunk the whole thing. Gately was careful to always leave her enough for a wake-up swallow. But this gesture of leaving some, Gately now realized, wasn't just filial kindness on his part: if she didn't have the wake-up swallow she wouldn't get off the red couch all day, and then there would be no new bottle that night.

This was at age 10 or maybe 11, as he now recalls. Most of the furniture was wrapped in plastic. The carpet was burnt-orange shag that the landlord kept saying he was going to take up and go to wood floors. The MP worked nights or else most nights went out, and then she'd take the plastic off the couch.

Why the couch had little protective doilies on the arms when it usually had a plastic cover on it Gately cannot recall or explain.

For a while in Beverly they had Nimitz the kitty.

This all came burpling greasily up into memory in the space of two or three weeks in May, and now more stuff steadily like dribbles up, for Gately to Touch.

Sober, she'd called him Bimmy or Bim because that's what she heard his little friends call him. She didn't know the neighborhood cognomen came from an acronym for "Big Indestructible Moron."

His head had been huge, as a child. Out of all proportion, though
with nothing especially Estonian about it, that he could see. He'd
been very sensitive about it—the head—but never told her not to call
him Bim. When she was drunk and conscious she called him her
Doshka or Dochka or something like that. Sometimes, well in the
bag himself, when he turned off the uncabled set and covered her
with the afghan, easing the mostly empty Stoli bottle back onto the
little *TV Guide* table by the bowl of darkening chopped peppers, his
unconscious Mom would groan and titter and call him her Doshka
and Good Sir Knight and last and only love, and ask him not to hit
her anymore.

In June he got in touch with memories that their front steps in
Beverly were a pocked cement painted red even in the pocks. Their
mailbox was part of a whole tract-housing complex's honeycomb of
mailboxes on a like small pole, brushed-steel and gray with a Postal
eagle on it. You needed a little key to get your mail out, and for a long
time he thought the sign on it said "US MAIL," as in *us* instead of U.S.
His Mom's hair had been dry blond-white with dark roots that never
lengthened or went away. No one tells you when they tell you you
have cirrhosis that eventually you'll all of a sudden start choking on
your own blood. This is called a *cirrhotic hemorrhage.* Your liver won't
process any more of your blood and it quote "shunts" the blood and
it goes up your throat in a high-pressure jet, is what they told him, is
why he'd first thought the MP'd come back and cut his Mom or
stabbed her, when he first came in, after football, his last season, at
age 17. She'd been diagnosed for years. She'd go to Meetings for a
few weeks, then drink on the couch, silent, telling him if the phone
rang she wasn't home. After a few weeks of this she'd spend a whole
day weeping, beating at herself as if on fire. Then she'd go back to
Meetings for a while. It was like a routine, a gerbil wheel. Her face
eventually began to swell and make her eyes piggy and her big breasts
pointed at the floor and she turned the deep yellow of quality squash.
This had all been part of the diagnosis of cirrhosis. At first Gately just
couldn't go, couldn't see her out there. Couldn't deal. Then after
some time passed he couldn't go because he couldn't face her and
try and explain why he hadn't come before now. Now ten years have
gone like that. Gately hadn't probably consciously thought of her
once for three years, before getting straight.

Right after their neighbor Mrs. Waite's body got found by the meter-guy, so he must have been 9, when his Mom was first diagnosed, Gately had gotten the diagnosis mixed up in his head with King Arthur. He'd ride a mop-handle horse and brandish a trashcan lid and a batteryless plastic Star Wars Light Saber and tell the neighborhood kids he was Sir Osis of Thuliver, most fearsomely loyal and fierce of Arthur's vessels. Since the summer now, when he mops Shattuck Shelter floors, he hears the clopaclopaclop he used to make with his big square tongue as Sir Osis then, riding.

And his dreams late that night, after the Braintree/Bob Death commitment, seem to set him under a sort of sea, at terrific depths, the water all around him silent and dim and the same temperature he is.

From
The Gospel According to Elvis

CHAPTER ONE

1   The book of the genealogy of Elvis, the son of Gladys, the daughter of Lovey Smith, the daughter of Winsome, the daughter of Grace, the daughter of Ezekia, the daughter of Yellowroot, and herein lies the mystery.

2   To go forth in those days meant to procreate. So Gladys went forth from the country to East Tupelo and found a silent man, likened to an empty vessel, an endless well with her own dark image at the bottom; and this man was called Vernon, meaning "to stir," meaning "spring," meaning a new beginning.

3   Vernon to himself was naught, but with the woman was more than himself, and he and the woman cleaved together. And a small house sprang up on the land, a hard land, given over to factories and machinery and chimneys and tools and debauchery. And Gladys was sore afraid.

4   She dreamed of shacks with children screaming from open windows, of muddy roads lined with worn shoes. The agony of her mind was cast abroad, and friends and neighbors wondered.

5   "Who is this woman ye hath brought among us?" the men muttered. Hanging his head, a head of bright cherub curls, Vernon did not reply, and kept all these things and pondered them in his heart.

6   Who knows the cause of each man's fortune or misfortune? This Vernon also pondered. And when no answer was forthcoming, he took the matter into his own hands, as one takes an unruly animal and tries to tame it and make it one's own.

7   And for this crime, he was snatched up and put in prison, during which time his fate swung back and forth like a pendulum. He, Vernon, was susceptible to wounds, to knife fights, to curses, to contagious thoughts. But the Lord was with him, and finally the Lord conquered.

8   He returned home, chastened, pearly-eyed, new-visioned. When he saw that his wife was with child, he sobbed, rejoicing.

9   Faithfulness was Gladys's way. The child of her belly would be his, though more Glorious, more Wonderful, the spirit of an age struggling with monsters re-risen.

10   And below these, the fox, the lobster, the ape, the owl, the leopard, the bobcat, the rattlesnake, the armadillo, the lost skull of a shepherd.

11   And Gladys, billowing into the air like an air-infested sail, cried out, cried for surcease, for deliverance.

12   And the first babe was stillborn, a sorrow for the poor mother but lo! another pushed itself out, a mirror-image of the first, more straggly, more meager, and this one op'd its mouth and cried.

13   So Jesse Garon was put in a shoebox and buried in an unmarked grave. And Elvis Aron lived, a shadow of the shadow, determined to be more than a shadow, determined to rise once more into the air from whence he came, a far planet some said; others claimed that a star arose in the heavens, and others that it darkened as in an eclipse.

CHAPTER TWO

1   "A race is ne'er won overnight," so Gladys saith, so Vernon agreed. Many days and nights rose and passed the horizon bringing many trials to be endured, many truths to be questioned.

2   Gladys, Vernon, and Elvis lived among themselves; and when they ventured abroad, it was always as one: one necessity, one charge, one purpose, which had to do with the son who was her Sun, who brightened her hours with his honesty and truthfulness and sincere ways.

3   And his world was stained with wonder: the winds and trees and creeks, the singing angels raising their voices to the Almighty in a great surge of rejoicing. And Elvis ran from his mother to join them, and stood wide-eyed while the sounds poured out, enclosing him, as in a cocoon, and he heard nothing else, not even his mother calling, softly scolding, her voice to him always soft, soft, though she herself was not entirely, and never to anyone else.

4   And people watching were amazed at the child who sat in church, rapt, listening to the notes soar around him while screams and shouts burst forth from the multitude, who did not hang back in their praise of the Lord. They praised foxes and grapes and floods and mountaintops; they praised Daniel and the Lions; they praised the peace that passeth understanding. Hark! Hark!

5   And Gladys kept all these things and pondered them in her heart.

6   At night she grieved for what might come to pass between her son and the Devil who lay in wait behind the darkest cloud and would bubble out of the ground at the first sign of sloth, when the cloth of the righteous would be rent and cast aside. And Vernon laughed at her fears.

7   "Doth Elvis not grow every day in stature and understanding?" he asked his wife as the three walked along the road to their tiny house, and later another house, and another, changing many times, for lack of money.

8   And Gladys softly cried while his father drew the boy's attention to the clear night and the cold stars. He called his wife's fears an "upheaval of the heart."

CHAPTER SIX

1   It soon came to pass that Elvis was given his first guitar: O strings! O finish! O sounds mournful and twangy!

2   And he slung this guitar around his neck and took it with him everywhere until it became part of his body, part of blood and membrane, cells and cuticles, his fingers nervously beating out a rhythm against the sides.

3   He went around seeking people to teach him how to play, to demonstrate chords and riffs and runs. And Uncle Vester showed him, and the preacher showed him, and a classmate showed him.

4   And he practiced hour after hour, sitting on his doorstep, naseling out lyrics like Tex and Gene and Roy, who used a guitar more often than a gun and whose picture-show voices turned the darkness into velvet, reminding him of the velvet angel on the velvet fountain over his Aunt Clettes's mantel.

5   And at home, he and his family would gather round the radio and listen to Hank Williams, to Roy Acuff and *The Great Speckled Bird*, to the jokes of Minnie Pearl who was surely named for Vernon's own mother, to Ernest Tubb and the Carter family. And the room glowed with their music.

6   Now not long after, Elvis and Gladys and Vernon moved from East Tupelo into the Negro section of the town.

7   In summer, with the doors of the houses flung open, he would stand listening to the gospel sounds spilling from kitchens and tiny parlors and on Sunday from the church at the end of the block where people dressed in flashy finery: wingtipped shoes, watchchains and fobs, hefty women in hot loud colors, bodies sashaying and swaying, and always with voices that plucked God out of the heavens.

8   And Elvis, sweaty and pimply-faced, without knowing why or wherefore, verily felt one of them.

CHAPTER TEN

1   Around this time, he had a number of auditions with local groups who greatly discouraged him from trying to be a singer, though the Lord called on him to persist, promising that he would at last prevail.

2   When the day of his anointing came and he walked into the recording room at Sun Studios, he was certain that the Lord would not forsake him.

3   For hours the tiny group of musicians tried out sounds, discarding song after song, phrase after phrase, and would have quit had not Sam Phillips, the studio owner, urged them on, never sure of what he was trying to achieve, though sensing that something was there, waiting to be coaxed to the surface.

4   And finally in a moment of hysteria and outrageous clowning, black and white at last emerged in one tumultuous rhythm, and Sam Phillips clapped his hands.

5   The song was called *That's All Right*, and it began to be played all over Memphis and everyone who knew Elvis and the Presley family was amazed.

6   "How is it," they asked themselves and each other, "how is it that a white boy from the wrong side of the tracks can arouse such feelings?" Even Gladys did not know the answer though she kept all these things and pondered them in her heart.

7   Meanwhile Elvis and his group played at Elks Clubs and bars and hole-in-the-wall nightspots where smoke lay leaden in the air, and he worked hard to make the songs rise above the beery talk. And Elvis's name rose, too, as did his record on the charts, until it began to be repeated over other parts of the South.

8   "O glory!" cried Gladys, all aquiver, and even Vernon came out of his stupor long enough to praise the Lord.

9   And Elvis appeared on the Grand Ole Opry, a longtime dream, then on Louisiana Hayride, where the audience stamped, hollered, and whistled every time he jerked his legs.

10   And Sam Phillips knew that what he was witnessing was luminous and rare, and joy ballooned in his chest till it felt close to bursting.

CHAPTER THIRTEEN

1   Now Elvis's stature swelled and swelled until it became a giant shadow over the whole land. And many were confused and ran to take cover while others threw up their arms shouting joyful hallelujahs. Still others saw fit to criticize, and a few of these had loud bellowing voices.

2   They accused Elvis of leading young people into sinful ways, of corrupting morals, of ungodly practices. When Gladys heard these things, she was sore afraid.

3   She begged her only-begotten son to forsake his golden fame and newly-coined fortune and return home forever and ever and ever. Forget the crowds, she pleaded; forget the autographs and interviews and concerts and records and jukeboxes.

4   Yet even as these words issued forth, they turned to water on her lips. And she saw clearly that Elvis was no longer hers but now belonged to the Colonel, who stood by grinning and rolling a cigar around in his mouth. And she moaned loudly and took to her bed.

5   Here her worst nightmares wore a new and more horrible aspect, as she watched her son constantly pacing up and down, exploding through the door and back again, gathering his buddies, who buzzed about him like honeybees, to be off in a zoom of thunder and reekings of the Devil's own smoky sputum.

6   And Gladys, in the privacy of her bedroom, gazed at herself in the mirror and saw how age had entrapped her: she was no longer the young wife who bore her trials with fortitude, nor the doting mother who dragged her boy with her wherever she went and kept scrapbooks of all his breathings and sighings.

7   She prayed to the Lord for comfort and He did answer her, though at first she recognized Him not. He sent a dream in which she and Vernon stood on the porch of a great mansion that rose on a hill above all the other houses. And in front was a pool that was driven by a ferocious wind into a huge wild ocean; suddenly she pointed toward one of the looming waves, and Elvis, who could not even swim, sailed over it in his bare feet. "Look!" she yelled, though Vernon, seeing nothing, laughed at her.

8   Awakening, she pondered this dream in the darkness of her own gloom. And whenever sadness came upon her, she railed at her doubts, thereby doubling her self-trouble by dwelling on much that was already doubled in her life.

9   Meanwhile Elvis stood at the pinnacle of his godlike fame, striding across the earth, not as a Colossus, but a jerking twisting figure that was likened to nothing ever seen before.

JOHN WATERS

Self-Portrait

Self-Portrait, 1994.
Ten chromogenic color prints, each 3 ½ x 5 in.

Secret Paragraphs About My Brother

There have been killings in Cambridge.

They want me to help them find the murderer, but I can't concentrate. The police feel there is a literary connection between the murders since all of those killed (except the nun from California) had belonged to an Upper West Side video club in Manhattan that had more than an ordinary number of writers as members. And at one time each had rented either *The Vanishing* or *Vertigo*.

It was the semester I dreamed of my son when he was sleepwalking. That was the winter before the summer of 1963 when my brother went for a drive in his car and was in the accident. I lay across the bed after I put my sons to sleep and suddenly painted one wall in the apartment red. My brother was in a coma for five months. When he woke, he was brain damaged and paralyzed. He died in 1972.

•

When I'm in Manhattan I retreat to the rooftop of my brownstone and read Russian classics—*Crime and Punishment* is my favorite. Some mornings I walk down Riverside Drive to 72nd Street. I often think about my brother.

Before he joined the Army, my brother went to Ohio State for a semester. He used to stand beneath my window in Baker Hall and practice his Spanish. Then one day he disappeared.

•

In Florence, July 1961, I didn't know that two summers from then there would be a terrible accident. I had given up writing plays. I had come to feel hopeless.

During that month, after I left American Express, I would often stop at the American Library and read *The New York Times*. One morning there was an exhibit in the window called *The Plays of Tennessee Williams*. It had been a long time since I had thought of Williams but now, as I stood staring at the volumes of *A Streetcar Named Desire*, *The Glass Menagerie*, *The Rose Tattoo*, I realized how much I still admired what Williams did. Perhaps I could write another play. The work on my desk that I had started in Ghana was an unclassified assortment of pages. I had no idea what form it would take but there was a character, Sarah, who was concerned about her thinning hair and another character, Clara, who spoke of her journey on an ocean liner. I had these characters speaking intensely of Queen Victoria and Patrice Lumumba. And I had a Jesus character who was speaking to my heroine. Perhaps I could write a play again, I thought as I walked back to Piazza Donatello. But no, I couldn't face that disappointment again. No matter how hard I had tried, I couldn't sustain a play in three acts like Williams and I couldn't achieve the density I so loved in Lorca.

Then one day, not long after I had returned to Rome to await the birth of my son, my husband arrived from Nigeria. We lived on Via Reno in a lovely apartment with a terrace that faced Rome. One morning, again on the way to American Express, I bought *The Times*. It was a very sunny morning. There was an article about Edward Albee, about the success of his one-act plays.

I had not thought of one-acts since I'd been about twenty-three. They seemed an oddity. But at that moment I decided I would try one one-act play and it would be the last thing I would write. I called it *Funnyhouse of A Negro*. The accident would take place the summer after its first performance.

•

In 1977, I was flying from London to Budapest (on the way to a theater conference) when I met a man who had been in Mannheim around the time of my brother's court martial (1956). He said he now worked for the American Embassy in Haiti. It was a night flight. My fellow passenger did not say why he was flying to Budapest, but he questioned me carefully on my role in the theater conference.

In Budapest soldiers with guns surrounded us as we deplaned in the December night. During our days at the Hotel Royal we were never alone. I bought my sons flutes and saw the Danube. In Berlin I went to see the Reichstag. I thought of Mannheim. Yet I was not able to go there. The conference office had booked me for Hamburg but I didn't go to Hamburg either. I stayed in Berlin and walked around the Alexanderplatz. And took a tour through the Black Forest.

Sometimes I think I still want to go to Mannheim. Would I have to disguise my motives in order to get my brother's old Army records? Perhaps I could unearth the story behind my brother's trial. I want to prove he was treated unfairly.

•

When he got married, his wife, Felicia, said to me, "I don't know where your brother is half the time."

"What do you mean?" (I always knew where my husband was.)

"I don't know where he is and don't know who his friends are," she said as we sat reading *House & Garden* and drinking Lipton's iced tea.

"Where did he go and who were his friends?" I asked my mother thirty years later.

"No one knew what he was doing half the time. He'd come in at three in the morning. I don't know where he'd been. He changed so after he came back from the Army," she replied.

After he got out of the Army he sought work in the psychiatric ward of Mt. Sinai Hospital. He was seldom without his white orderly's jacket.

•

"Was your brother's nickname Charlie?" asked the undertaker at my father's funeral.

"I never knew my brother had a nickname," I said. "We called him ———. And what made you think of my brother?" (He had been dead three years, and it was a different undertaker who had buried him.) This undertaker was a son of one of my father's oldest friends. My parents married in his house in Dayton, Ohio in 1930.

"We were talking last night about your family and someone said, didn't Mr. —— have a son called 'Charlie'? He knew it was a nickname."

I said I'd never heard that but I'd ask my mother.

When I got home from the funeral parlor I asked her. She stared at me.

"I never heard that," she said. "I don't know anything about a 'Charlie.'"

Today I still wonder if he had a life as "Charlie" and if she knew.

•

This reminded me of years ago and Rosemary and our Italian neighborhood. One summer evening I was playing jacks on the steps when I saw my friends run past my house toward the vacant lot on Signet.

"Aren't you coming?" someone said. "—— and Rosemary are getting married."

I knew nothing of this and arrived at the edge of the field of weeds to see Rosemary and my brother standing before a boy I'd never seen. Rosemary was in her communion dress and my brother in his playsuit.

Just as I arrived they ran deeper into the field and disappeared.

"They went on their honeymoon," someone screamed.

When my brother came home toward dark he stopped and stood in front of me at the porch steps.

"Don't tell Mother and Daddy I'm married," he said.

He was six and I was nine.

•

Cars united them. It was a car in which my brother met his disfiguration. (He was driving to see Felicia.) And it was in a car that my father's second wife was instantly killed in an accident that killed his spirit. The biggest argument my father and brother had was over a car—the silver-colored Kaiser. My brother wanted to drive it to a party. My father said he couldn't take the car.

They stood in the center of the living room yelling. I ran down the stairs from my room. My father was small. Was my brother about to knock him down? I started crying. I could see my father was afraid. I feared the worst. My mother was in Maryland on a trip. I was about to run onto the front porch and call a neighbor when suddenly they stopped yelling. My father threw the Kaiser keys on the floor at my brother's feet.

Soon after, my brother joined the Army.

It was spring when my brother left for Germany. He and Felicia arrived on the train from Ohio on the day the movie *Guys and Dolls* opened in New York. I wanted to go to 50th Street and Broadway. Brando was playing Sky Masterson and *The New York Post* said he would be at the opening.

•

Often I dream of my father pulling the silver-colored Kaiser into the driveway, the same silver Kaiser in which my brother came back from a drive late one night with blood on the fender. He said he'd hit a dog. It remained a mystery. There were so many mysteries surrounding my brother. During those years, he and my mother would often go into the bathroom and close the door.

"Mother, I want to talk to you," he'd mumble and into the bathroom they'd go and run the water loudly. I don't know what they talked about.

My mother would emerge, minutes later, and run into her bedroom. Often I could hear her sobbing.

"What's wrong?" I'd say, trying to open her closed door.

Once, months later, she said, "Your brother may have to go to court."

"Court?"

"I don't want to talk about it." And she walked away.

•

"Mind your own business," my brother would say whenever I'd ask what was wrong. "Mind your own business."

He died without telling me anything.

An Elegy of Mimnermus

(An Imitation)

How much joy is left in life
Without the blessing of foam-
Born Aphrodite? Let me die now
That I can no longer have love
Secrets and the gifts of desire
And the pleasures of soft beds.
These were the blossomings of
Youth, giving happiness both
To young men and their lovers.
But age brings aches and bad
Smells to the man who has
Grown old. It makes evil
Flourish in his body and
Mind. It wears down the heart.
For him the warmth of sunlight
Is diminished. Children fear
Him and women despise him.
Cruel is the treatment with
Which the gods punish old age.

Mardi Gras

Venice, Italy, 1995

The first time I saw Mardi Gras in Venice was about five years ago, when I was invited there by Gianni Agnelli to see the Andy Warhol retrospective that he was putting on at Palazzo Grassi. It was incredibly warm that year and I took my first gondola trip and it was amazing: I didn't hear the crowd at all; I was just gliding through the city on this silent boat, and suddenly I'd pass under a bridge where all these people were doing "freezes"—standing completely still in a fixed pose—in their masks. You'd see whole families dressed in similar costumes posing together. And there was a fog that drifted through it all. It was the most surreal experience I have ever had. I went back this year because I'd convinced my friend, Giovanni Volpi, to go to it. Even though he's a Venetian count, he had never seen Mardi Gras, because his family had always gone to Switzerland or somewhere else when the tourists came flooding in.

The first Mardi Gras I ever saw was in New Orleans, when I was shooting *Easy Rider*, and it was very intense. The whole idea of Mardi Gras is that you can sin as much as you want because you're going to have to spend the next forty days repenting for Lent anyway. In New Orleans, it's a different experience. It's very noisy and very violent. Fights break out all the time and people get shot or stabbed. But I've never felt any kind of violence in Venice. It's more sophisticated and very laid back. There are no cars, no honking or traffic jams. And the masks are incredibly refined. The costumes have been passed down through families for generations.

Photographing it was complicated. Other photographers would get in the way. Sometimes I included them on purpose, to capture the reality of the scene. Other times the people I was shooting would recognize me and start poking each other and pointing at me. I didn't wear a costume. I went as Dennis Hopper.

—Dennis Hopper

The Fishing Man

An old partridge flies home sluggishly
towards Tatatóváros. He was out hunting:
he was hunted.
> Sándor Márai: NOVEMBER (Flea market)

I still saw him,
but he was no longer fishing,

he was too old
and there was no place for it,

among ourselves we called him uncle,

he wore white linen trousers,
a white linen shirt,
and he sat on the bench in front of his house,

everything about him was white
except his sandals,
his clothes white,
his hair white,
spruce and clean,
like in an old peasant play,
all that was missing was the freshly painted picket fence in front
of him,

he was a widower,
his wife already in the cemetery,

now and then he went into the house,
puttered around a bit,
then came out again,

ambled along slowly under the low eaves
on the natural stone footway
to the end of the house
and back,
with his palm he carefully tapped back the pieces of rye straw that
                                                    had slipped out,

his was the last thatched roof in the village,

but generally he didn't do anything,
only sat
and listened,
smoked his pipe
and looked straight ahead,
as if the earth were water,
and he saw fish in it,

we always fell silent
when we got there,

we even forgot to greet him,
as though we hadn't wanted to disturb him,
as though we had felt
that he was fishing in his memory
and would have liked to catch something
before departing, like the pond,
which had been drained in his lifetime,

although we didn't know
that he was the fishing man,

I was told so years later by my father,
when he was already dead
and the house too had been pulled down.

Soldiers' Graves

Ever since I can remember,
they had always been there,
in our garden, next to the cemetery,
they were lined up in the potato field,
packed in side by side,

they formed a long, narrow island on the flats,
the waves of plantings lapping against them,

at first I thought
children were lying under the mounds,
they were so short, so tiny,

they were no special trouble,
we simply detoured around them
and were glad
that we had that much less to hoe,

only in the spring they were a bit in the way,
we had to be careful then
that we didn't plow into them,
or let the horse trample them,

in summer we sickled the grass from their borders,
but we didn't take it home for the cattle,
we threw it into the hedgerow,

once every year, on All Souls' Day, we'd weed them thoroughly,
put them in order,
and place lighted candles on them,
as if they were relatives,
but only one on each,
because they cost money,

sometimes I tried to relate them to the bloodthirsty beasts in
                                                    Soviet films,
but it didn't work,
I couldn't take offense at them,
my friend Miki always came to mind,
whose father hadn't come home from the war
and might be buried like this somewhere in Russia,
or even worse than this,

then, as the years slipped by,
they sank deeper and deeper
and got smaller and smaller,
the wooden crosses rotted and got lost, along with the foreign
                                                    names,
I began to mix up the old acquaintances,
Kurt for Hans,
Hermann for Jürgen,
Otto for Reiner,
until finally I completely forgot
who was who, when he was born,
and how old he was when he fell,

we paid less and less attention to them,
we realized we couldn't look after them forever,
we couldn't hold back decay,

sometimes we were thoughtless enough
to sit on them,
or step on them,
although we still kept them in mind,

in Fifty-six, when we swapped the garden for a building lot,
they were still there,
but when the vacated field was annexed to the cemetery,
and, so to speak, they took their rightful places,
they were mercilessly churned up, even leveled,
a new funeral home was built,
a little open area was wanted in front of it,
and that's where it was,

since then they've been unmarked,
but those resting below are no longer alone,
in the meantime they've acquired many companions,
a whole villageful of civilians moved in,
and it got so crowded
that the cemetery had to be enlarged once again.

Translated from the Hungarian by Bruce Berlind
with Mária Kőrösy

Bird Music

The composer Olivier Messiaen's approach to his own work varied with time and with the kinds of students he was dealing with. For the "bird works," we have an invaluable source: a tape recording of various classes on the Catalogue d'oiseaux, *a vast piano cycle that dates from 1956–1958. The recording was made by Francois-Bernard Mâche, probably in the spring of 1959, and a copy was placed in the I.N.A. sound archives in Paris.

In a way, Messiaen was offering a course in ornithology, complete with illustrated editions and color plates. After describing the bird and relating the circumstances under which it was observed, he read out, in a declamatory style, the introductory text he had prepared for each piece in the cycle. The piece in question was then played by the pianist Yvonne Loriod, who was invited for the occasion, and as she played the composer explained out loud the correspondences between the music and the introductory text. For the composer, the text was absolutely inextricable from the music and virtually supplanted any other kind of analysis. This tape shows us a professor who is relaxed with his students, who are fairly attentive (especially during the playing of the pieces) and not at all embarrassed to ask questions or make comments. In short, the tape shows us everything that the students were not able to mark down in their notebooks. (The passages in italics were read by Messiaen from his own introductory text.)

—*Jean Boivin*

We shall begin with the most difficult of all the pieces, the most difficult to understand: *Le Merle de roche* (*The Rock Thrush*) [the tenth piece in the collection]. Although it is called a *merle* (blackbird), make no mistake: it is actually a *monticole* (rock thrush), a bird that lives in the rocks, and is somewhere between a blackbird and a redstart, not strictly a blackbird. It is a very difficult bird to reach or to see, and I had a great deal of difficulty trying to hear it. I saw it twice, both times in complicated circumstances. . . . In Latin it is called *Monticola saxatilis*. . . . It is an extremely beautiful bird, beautiful for its song as well as for its plumage. . . . As you see, it has brown wings—and a blue head, grayish blue, and the throat, breast, stomach, and tail are an orangish color, but a brilliant orange. [In the photograph] we see the bird on top of a crag. It is an extremely timid bird, hard to find because it is always in rugged country, but if you are lucky enough to find one, it will be out in the open because it likes to sing while perched in plain view showing its handsome orange breast.

[After describing the respective colorings of the male and female, Messiaen shows other images and then, in a firm, grave, and solemn voice, reads his introductory text. His tone of voice returns to normal for the explanations and then becomes serious again when he resumes reading.] *Month of May. The Hérault. Le Cirque de Mourèze* [a mountain valley in southern France]. A magnificent place, I'm going to show you photographs of it—*chaos de dolomies.* (For the foreigners here, *dolomies* are limestone cliffs worn away by erosion. The name comes from the geologist Dolomieux, and there is a whole region in Italy called the Dolomites because of this.) *Fantastically shaped crags. Night, moonlight. Towering over the other cliffs, an immense stone hand!* (Imagine a hand perhaps forty meters high. This is absolutely true. There is a kind of hand, no one ever noticed it, but. . .) *Toward the end of night, the great horned owl hoots powerfully and gravely.* (This is a huge owl, an owl like this, as big as an eagle.) —*Its female* (the female of the great horned owl) *responds with muffled percussions: a sinister hilarity whose rhythm merges with the frightened heartbeat.* The female emits a kind of laugh, like this: [Messiaen makes a sound by forcefully expelling air]. It's frightening. *Break of day: cries of jackdaws. Then the redstart begins its monotonous song: in the middle of the strophe, a noise, reminiscent of shaken pearls, crumpled paper, a whisper of silk. The cliffs are terrifying. Final jackdaw cries. End of twilight: the great*

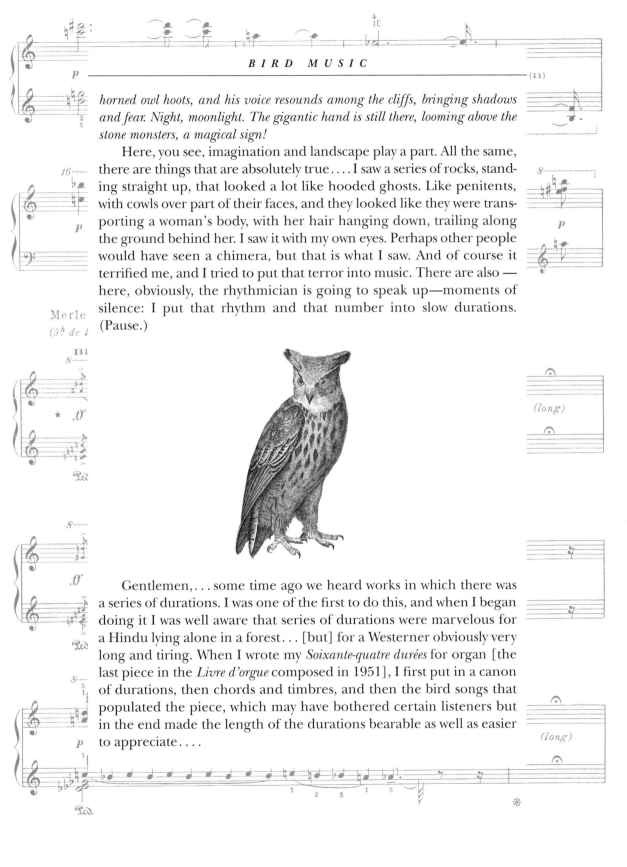

horned owl hoots, and his voice resounds among the cliffs, bringing shadows and fear. Night, moonlight. The gigantic hand is still there, looming above the stone monsters, a magical sign!

Here, you see, imagination and landscape play a part. All the same, there are things that are absolutely true.... I saw a series of rocks, standing straight up, that looked a lot like hooded ghosts. Like penitents, with cowls over part of their faces, and they looked like they were transporting a woman's body, with her hair hanging down, trailing along the ground behind her. I saw it with my own eyes. Perhaps other people would have seen a chimera, but that is what I saw. And of course it terrified me, and I tried to put that terror into music. There are also — here, obviously, the rhythmician is going to speak up—moments of silence: I put that rhythm and that number into slow durations. (Pause.)

Gentlemen,... some time ago we heard works in which there was a series of durations. I was one of the first to do this, and when I began doing it I was well aware that series of durations were marvelous for a Hindu lying alone in a forest... [but] for a Westerner obviously very long and tiring. When I wrote my *Soixante-quatre durées* for organ [the last piece in the *Livre d'orgue* composed in 1951], I first put in a canon of durations, then chords and timbres, and then the bird songs that populated the piece, which may have bothered certain listeners but in the end made the length of the durations bearable as well as easier to appreciate....

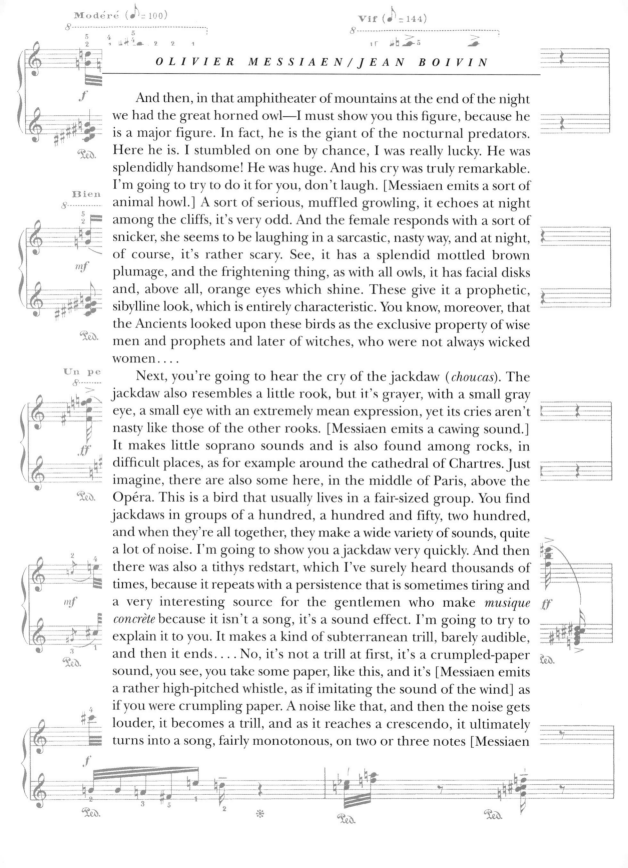

And then, in that amphitheater of mountains at the end of the night we had the great horned owl—I must show you this figure, because he is a major figure. In fact, he is the giant of the nocturnal predators. Here he is. I stumbled on one by chance, I was really lucky. He was splendidly handsome! He was huge. And his cry was truly remarkable. I'm going to try to do it for you, don't laugh. [Messiaen emits a sort of animal howl.] A sort of serious, muffled growling, it echoes at night among the cliffs, it's very odd. And the female responds with a sort of snicker, she seems to be laughing in a sarcastic, nasty way, and at night, of course, it's rather scary. See, it has a splendid mottled brown plumage, and the frightening thing, as with all owls, it has facial disks and, above all, orange eyes which shine. These give it a prophetic, sibylline look, which is entirely characteristic. You know, moreover, that the Ancients looked upon these birds as the exclusive property of wise men and prophets and later of witches, who were not always wicked women. . . .

Next, you're going to hear the cry of the jackdaw (*choucas*). The jackdaw also resembles a little rook, but it's grayer, with a small gray eye, a small eye with an extremely mean expression, yet its cries aren't nasty like those of the other rooks. [Messiaen emits a cawing sound.] It makes little soprano sounds and is also found among rocks, in difficult places, as for example around the cathedral of Chartres. Just imagine, there are also some here, in the middle of Paris, above the Opéra. This is a bird that usually lives in a fair-sized group. You find jackdaws in groups of a hundred, a hundred and fifty, two hundred, and when they're all together, they make a wide variety of sounds, quite a lot of noise. I'm going to show you a jackdaw very quickly. And then there was also a tithys redstart, which I've surely heard thousands of times, because it repeats with a persistence that is sometimes tiring and a very interesting source for the gentlemen who make *musique concrète* because it isn't a song, it's a sound effect. I'm going to try to explain it to you. It makes a kind of subterranean trill, barely audible, and then it ends. . . . No, it's not a trill at first, it's a crumpled-paper sound, you see, you take some paper, like this, and it's [Messiaen emits a rather high-pitched whistle, as if imitating the sound of the wind] as if you were crumpling paper. A noise like that, and then the noise gets louder, it becomes a trill, and as it reaches a crescendo, it ultimately turns into a song, fairly monotonous, on two or three notes [Messiaen

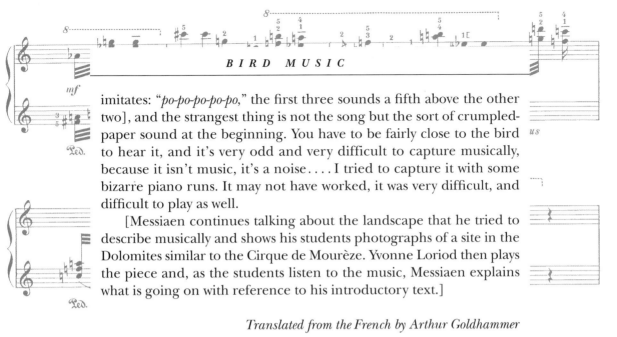

imitates: "*po-po-po-po-po*," the first three sounds a fifth above the other two], and the strangest thing is not the song but the sort of crumpled-paper sound at the beginning. You have to be fairly close to the bird to hear it, and it's very odd and very difficult to capture musically, because it isn't music, it's a noise. . . . I tried to capture it with some bizarre piano runs. It may not have worked, it was very difficult, and difficult to play as well.

[Messiaen continues talking about the landscape that he tried to describe musically and shows his students photographs of a site in the Dolomites similar to the Cirque de Mourèze. Yvonne Loriod then plays the piece and, as the students listen to the music, Messiaen explains what is going on with reference to his introductory text.]

Translated from the French by Arthur Goldhammer

(les Choucas)

Un peu vif (♪=120)

The Birds

Put the niggers over there, he said, indicating one of his white, floor-to-ceiling bookcases that was literally littered with niggers, or what he sometimes referred to as "niggerati," a term invented by the folklorist and writer Zora Neale Hurston. "Niggerati" was how the poet, novelist, playwright, and instructor Owen Dodson used to describe the Negro fag intellectuals whose reflexive, sentimental race consciousness comprised the ideology that informed the Harlem Renaissance.

The books written by the men and women Owen also referred to as "niggerish," and whom he asked me to put "over there," had been published in the '20s, '30s, and '40s; those books had gone the way many literary vogues do—abandoned on someone's dusty shelf, book jackets tattered, with personal inscriptions as faint as the faint ideas expounded in them. In Owen's youth, the literary vogue had focused on the "New Negro," his or her "story." The aesthetic of the New Negro celebrated, in folklore and poetry, novels and plays, these authors' misbegotten Southern or Middle American pasts. The philosopher Alain Locke, who coined the phrase "New Negro," wrote in 1925 : "There is ample evidence of a New Negro in the latest phases of social change and progress, but still more in the internal world of the Negro mind and spirit." The New Negro writers' internal worlds were never revealed in their work, which did not examine

Opposite: Owen Dodson, circa 1948.

141

their abiding intellectual and emotional curiosity about European culture; nor did it speak of their aspiration to be absorbed by that culture, where they would find new privilege as the objects of curiosity. Nor did their work examine the deeper exigencies of the mind, the self. The work of New Negro writers such as Zora Neale Hurston, Langston Hughes, Alain Locke, and Countee Cullen—all of whom Owen had known—did not explain why or how they had adopted "race" as a frame for their work; it did not explain how they constructed that frame out of fear—the fear that, should they be divested of rhetoric, they would no longer exist—or, at the very least, risked being absorbed by the existential debate that consumes every writer: Who Am I? Instead, they chose ideology, the sanctimonious: As A Black, I Am, or Was, or Should Be.

As New Negroes, they defended their right to be "oppressed"; as agents of the rhetoric of oppression, they were insistent on their "correctness." Often this position resulted in bad prose and (far more often) bad poetry. The New Negro supported the continuum of white power by bemoaning, on the page, its existence. And, for this performance, the New Negroes were roundly applauded by white publishers and patrons, who rewarded them with stipends, book deals, and no criticism whatsoever. What the New Negro was: a model of repressed and repressive middle-class aspirations.

These New Negroes were children hungry for the comfort of group ideology (or therapy). They sought validation everywhere, even as they took up their pens to inscribe feebly in those now-forgotten books: "To Our Brother, Owen Dodson." Knowing all of this but not voicing it, Owen said *Put the niggers over there* with irony. He also said it to those critics and scholars whom he eyed with disdain because they took the period's infantile cultural production seriously, and because they remained willfully ignorant of the Harlem Renaissance's true significance: as the moment when Negro social life devolved from Negro to black.

I met Owen Dodson, this collector of traces of '30s and '40s Negro social life, through a woman friend of his whom he had known since high school, and who was also a friend of my mother's. For a fee, this woman taught poetry and piano to "gifted" children interested in either. I got a scholarship. I didn't study poetry there; instead I studied the woman's matted wig, her bad teeth, and her intractable bewilderment: her bewilderment over her continued connection to her husband, who had gone blind during the war after refusing to be treated for syphilis with penicillin; her bewilderment over not being able to manage the mean and hungry dogs she kept locked in the attic; her bewilderment at young people like myself, whose ambition would consume what she had to offer and carry them on to the next person they would need to consume in order to become something other than themselves. This woman said: I want to send you to my friend Owen's house; he wants to give away books. I was thirteen then. It was 1974.

On the afternoon we first met, Owen showed me a number of photographs that had been taken of him when he was young. Through these photographs, I was able to see how much I resembled him. We also resembled one another in our ability to charm, and in what we falsely projected: relatively easy access to our internal selves. In order to be liked, we had both learned how to please an audience. By the time I met Owen, he was said to have become exhausted by his charm. In order to be charming, he drank and drink energized him socially, unless he drank too much, which was most of the time. At the time, I had just begun to be confused by my attraction to reflection (writing) and to being social. We were in love at first sight.

He took the American Negro's xenophobic interest in my West Indian background. I took an interest in his connection to Negro glamour and social life. I learned that afternoon that much of Negro social custom had been built on skewered European social mores— in the overlaying of European formality of dress with visual rhetoric (the oversized tiger lily attached to the lapel in place of a discreet boutonniere; the heavily pomaded hair instead of a crisp bob). I also learned that the principle of Negro style was "making do," and then flaunting it. This was all as disjunctive and foreign to me as the images I had seen of moneyed Chinese wearing European dress during the '20s.

Two years after that, my ambition found me a frequent visitor to Owen's home carrying out his command to *Put the niggers over there*, in the bookcase opposite his bed. There was dust on the books. His lips were like impacted dust. When he said: *Put the niggers over there*, he pointed with a long, crooked finger with a blunt nail—his left index finger—which was heavy with one silver ring, indicating where the books should be put. I put the niggerish books on the shelf. I was fifteen. Already I knew that the India ink inscriptions, "To

Owen Dodson, cher maître," and so on, were the faded sentiments of friends he had not seen for many years. But the impulse to befriend and to garner the respect of students had not faded enough from his memory for him to resist his impulse to nurture other people, other writers. He was a pedant. He could not trust his mind to isolation.

The dim yellow light filled with dust motes circled next to the nigger books whose inscriptions trembled with age. To one side of the bookcase were letters stored in letter boxes from many people he used to amuse, people who no longer received him socially since he had been crippled by arthritis and had had two hip operations. He was incoherent half the time. His small hand with its blunt nail curled around the necks of liquor bottles. Sometimes, after waking, or when he was ready to receive students, his hand also wrapped around the necks of Listerine bottles, still in their green wrappers. He gargled in the vain hope that Listerine would make his tongue and teeth desirable to all the young men who would never allow Owen to call them lover, many of whom pitied his shrunken, heavily cologned figure just enough to let his gray-haired head graze their young and wide-with-ambition shoulders, but never enough to let his hand graze their crotches.

By the time I met him, he rarely said what he thought. Nor did he think much before he spoke. His speech was reflexive and articulate but not necessarily thoughtful. He was slowly turning into a dust mote. Often he bounced happily on the air expelled by the laughter of friends and hangers-on, or of loyal former students from Howard University, where he had been dean of the university's Drama Department. He told many of the same stories many times. He told how, after he had committed himself to directing the first production ever of James Baldwin's *The Amen Corner*, at Howard in 1954 ("The deans said, 'This play will put the Speech Department back fifty years!'"), Baldwin arrived in Washington for the premiere and quickly encamped himself in Owen's home, followed by his lover, and his enormous family, who proceeded to eat Owen out of house and home. "Niggers!" Owen exclaimed at the end of this story, which was meant to illustrate his own character, his tale of kindnesses unpaid, debts tallied. His dusty lips began to flake as he reached to pour himself another drink and another story.

Once I put my tongue in his mouth after he had vomited into his soup plate, during a dinner he had prepared with the help of his older sister, Edith, with whom he lived. The dinner was in honor of the many colored people who still considered Owen's home on West 51st Street a landmark of Negro style. The people I saw there were the actors Roscoe Lee Brown and Ruby Dee and Ossie Davis; the novelists Margaret Walker and Toni Morrison ("She was Howard's beauty queen one year!"), and others he would eventually put "over there" on the shelf. Vomiting into his soup plate, he sputtered and choked while his guests pretended not to notice, as did Edith, who was smaller than her brother and more suspicious. She suffered from a sexual despair that was the result of a first marriage gone bad and from her self-perceived homeliness, which endowed her with the patience and moral fortitude necessary to read John Galsworthy's *The Forsyte Saga* over and over again, as well as an ability to ignore her brother's repeated emotional indiscretions: the way he elevated every male student to protegé, and, eventually, to husband.

I took the plate swimming with Listerine and liquor and soup remains and flushed it down the toilet. He moved away from the table. He had a walker, a silver walker, that helped him clink clunk down the endless red-carpeted hallway, its walls hung with one large painting of San Sebastian and one large drawing of Icarus, falling; these images represented his literary imagination, just as the wooden posters cramming the dining room walls, announcing performances long past—Katharine Cornell in *The Doctor's Dilemma* and Charles Trenet on Columbia Records—represented his attachment to grand theater and bohemianism.

Although many, many people knew what Owen's intellectual and aesthetic tastes were, they never discussed the absence of those tastes from his written work, where he forfeited his vision for the sake of Negro respectability, writing what he felt should be said instead of what he wanted to say, as in his "Poem for Pearl's Dancers":

On my back they've written history, Lord,
On my back they've lashed out hell....
When my children get to reading, Lord,
On my back they'll read my tale.

Such sentiments were literally employable. In 1944, Owen served as the executive secretary for the Committee for Mass Education in Race Relations, intended to help "abolish" Hollywood's stereotypical view of blacks. He was anthologized in *The Book of Negro Folklore*, edited by Langston Hughes, in 1958. Because, by the time I met him, most of his friends were his former students, he never admitted how lost he was when he wrote. In his second novel, *Come Home Early, Child*, which he wrote in 1958 although it wasn't published until 1977, Owen's characters shrink beneath the glare of the grease paint he rubs on their cheeks for effect. He was too lazy intellectually to look for the metaphors best suited to express the meaning in his poems, plays, or novels; he relied instead on hackneyed "poetic" language to create character.

His work was an interesting example of a tired genre; it was the product of a *deliberately* "black" writer, whose primary talent was spent seeking out an audience to view the chip on his shoulder, a chip darker than the author himself. Owen wrote:

Slaves: *Laughing*
Ya gonna discover one of these days
That the white man got two dozen ways to lie an cheat
To conjure with deceit.

Many of the poems that appear in his first collection, *Powerful Long Ladder* (1946), imitated the dialect his white predecessors had used in their work, poets such as Edgar Lee Masters and Carl Sandburg. Owen's imitations of those poets who appropriated black syntax— itself a linguistic metaphor for the outsiderness they felt—was as ill-fitting as Uncle Jimbilly's wooly, unconditional love and speech in Katherine Anne Porter's short story, *The Witness*. It is difficult to account for the poems Owen wrote in dialect: he was born and raised in Brooklyn. But dialect he used, hoping to become authentic in his "blackness" rather than distinct in his Negroness. From "Black Mother Praying":

Listen, Lord, they ain't nowhere for black mothers to turn.
Won't You plant Your Son's goodness in this land
Before it too late?
Set Your stars of sweetness twinklin over us like winda lamps
Before it too late?

By the time I met him, he was no longer interested in writing. He had already begun to move away from the expansive interior places writing could have taken him to. He was interested in people, the social life his "name" generated, and in representing those parts of his style he could still access through his flirtatious and exotic clothes.

In the twilight blue of his room, Owen collapsed on his bed; he had one real hip and one large shoe with a lift in it. I took off his brocaded vest and then turned on his bedside lamp; gravity pulled his brown skin back; his face was suddenly as smooth as a death mask. There was the smell of urine in the room. A bottle clanked under the bed; he had been drinking alone before dinner, dust motes floating above him, and history floating above him too, which he could not keep out of his room, not even with the heavy drapes that covered the windows of his thirteenth-floor penthouse on West 51st Street. Those curtains locked it in, like a neurasthenic's will. His apartment was located across from a townhouse to which was attached a neon sign that read on one side, "Jesus Saves," and on the other, "Sin Will Find You Out." I removed the trousers and vest he had put on with great effort hours before, when slumped in his bed, he had applied a hair tonic to smooth back his hair and comb his mustache. He made his wobbly way to the dinner table where he told one story ("When Edith and I were little, we had to recite in church, and quote the scriptures. Edith's quote: 'Jesus wept.'") before throwing up in his plate and making his way back to the bed and reaching up for my face and kissing my mouth, whispering, "Do what you want," in my ear, just as I started unbuttoning his shirt. The bedroom door was slightly ajar. I closed it and bent over him, as happy for this moment of displeasure as I was happy for every moment of pleasure. His teeth clenched as I clenched his arms. I was fifteen. He was older than my mother but just as committed to the experience of pain as she was, just as resolute in his commitment to the internal visions the experience of pain affords. Lying with him in this way, I heard my mother's voice—my imagination's radio—and began to understand that what I could give to Owen in moments like these I would never live long enough to use in support of my mother: my monstrous ambition, which she had no interest in, but which accounted, in part, for my being with Owen. With Owen, I was farther into the world than my mother and sisters had ever been. Also: his home displaced the squalor I lived in, but did not sacrifice the narrative of oppression that inspired poems like Owen's "Black Mother Praying." For years I emulated the ideology that served as the poem's foundation: the search for a secular God, a God that black theologian James Cone has called a "god of the oppressed." In Owen's arms, I learned many things. I learned how to think. When I began thinking, he grew angry because it wasn't long before I found out the sin in his work: his inability to convey intimacy. He bypassed his own individual experience for the *gemütlich* feeling of group oppression. He became part of a movement.

But even within movements, hierarchies exist. As one of the disenfranchised, Owen was less popular than his *bête noire*, James Baldwin, in whose work one finds the pathos that accounts for the continued popularity of Charles Dickens's *David Copperfield* and *Oliver Twist*. Baldwin's *Notes of a Native Son* simply places the articulate Dickensian orphan in thrall to a black god—Father, with his inherited power to "oppress": "In my mind's eye I could see [my father],... hating and fearing every living soul including his children who had betrayed him, too, by reaching toward the world which had despised him.... I began to wonder what it could have felt like for such a man to have had nine children whom he could barely feed." It was galling for Owen to know that Baldwin began writing *Notes of a Native Son*, the essay that established him, in Owen's home, fortified by Owen's liquor and attention. And it would have upset Owen to know that the one book of his that I borrowed and never returned was Baldwin's *Nobody Knows My Name*, in which he writes about his relationship with his mentor, Richard Wright. I liked the book less for what Baldwin had to say than for its dust jacket. The dust jacket showed Baldwin through the grid of a broken window standing in a pile of inner-city rubble. He projects a look of pathos meant to chip away at the invulnerability of the general reader. I have always been mesmerized by how writers manage to theatricalize their isolation for the camera. Perhaps he appropriated this look of defenseless reason from the work of Harlem Renaissance writers. I do know that the poet Countee Cullen had been an instructor of Baldwin's at DeWitt Clinton High School. In *Alas Poor Richard*, Baldwin states: "[Wright's] work was an immense liberation and revelation for me. He became my ally, and my witness, and alas! my father."

I did not consider Owen my father and his work was not an immense liberation for me. What I loved and admired in Owen was his ability to project himself larger than any actor I had ever seen, and to hurtle me back to the '40s, the years of his greatest social success. When Owen took me to one restaurant or another that had been popular during that era, he would order a repast that had been chic then: shrimp cocktails and martinis. I especially loved being with him those nights, in that frozen time, which had occurred long before our friendship began. Eating with Owen was like eating his curiously shaped history. Like most great teachers, he opened up the world for me. Like most people, he resented it when I left him to find what I could in it.

I entered Owen's mouth and his liquor-swollen tongue made a sound against mine. He was grateful for my size, which embarrassed me—I was bigger but tried to walk small, talk small, leave the room without being in it, because I hated being physically larger than my admiration for him, which was considerable; also, my large body seemed like too obvious a metaphor for my ambition, which was also considerable.

But to his mind, my size made me a man in relation to his woman, his quivering vulnerability and position on the bed, which was one of acceptance. Being larger, I was immediately thought of by him and, in years to come, by many others, as forceful, someone whose sole physical purpose is to enter this body of acceptance again and again, becoming the spine that encloses closeness and encases intimacy; and there we were, with my spine bent over his breathing, like the spine of a tent, his skin like the folds of a tent. He was my first woman.

He did not say what he thought about this moment, or any other. He was always ambivalent about using language to describe sexual pleasure. He had despised his body from his earliest years as the youngest child of a family once considered one of Brooklyn's finest. His father, Nathaniel, had been a journalist, editor of the syndicated weekly *Afro-American Page*. But his family dissolved quickly when he was still a boy, due to the early deaths of his mother and father. By the time he was an adolescent, he had lost five brothers and sisters and was left with only two older sisters, Edith and Lillian, and his much beloved brother, Kenneth. Lillian, the eldest, was stern in her Negro reverence for education and discipline. She supported her siblings on her schoolteacher's salary. She wore sensible shoes; the sound of her heels clacked in his head forever. He was especially close to his brother, Kenneth ("I should have slept with him; we loved each other so."), but Kenneth died young ("When he died, I lay in a darkened bedroom; I screamed."). The entire family was stunned by its despair in relation to sexuality. And Kenneth's death made Owen forever a romantic. As such, he was impatient with intellection, or any process that intruded on the drama he erected around dying—"Sorrow is the only faithful one," he once wrote. He generally preferred imagining death even to physical intimacy. Kenneth had been the true romantic or poet—Owen said.

Owen reached up and circled my neck with his hands. I lifted him slightly and bit both nipples on his chest. *Put the niggers over there,* he said, perhaps not thinking. So little in those niggerish books was the result of thinking. That language was produced for an audience, not for the writers themselves. This is what Owen surrounded himself with and one reason (maybe) why he spoke without thinking.

He went to Bates College in Maine, and received his Master of Fine Arts degree in theater from Yale. After Yale: various teaching appointments before becoming a professor at Howard, where he staged Ibsen and got grants and so forth, and was so seemingly welcoming of talents greater than his own—the composer David Amram, Baldwin, et al.—that he filled himself up with more company and fewer words. His books of poetry—*The Confession Stone* and *Powerful Long Ladder*—and novels—*Boy at the Window, Come Home Early, Child*—and plays—*The Confession Stone, Divine Comedy*—are less about matching words to thoughts than about filling up his resume and the ghastly Negro void to "achieve" up. He was filled up with—what? My tongue, from time to time. "Oh," he said, as I tried to remove his one large shoe—enjoying the visual incongruity of things: one big shoe off, the normal shoe still on. Dust motes flew as his fingers fluttered around my face. Behind those fingers I thought: *One day, I will be as old as he is now, with someone who cares as little or as much as I do now.* For as long as I knew him (I left him when I was nineteen) our relationship was that of the pedant and his student consumed with ambition. What the pedant knows: his ambitious student will stop at nothing in order to learn how to be himself; he will stop at nothing, not even at inhaling his teacher's vomit-smeared breath, as penance for the guilt he feels in wanting this more than anything else: to become a self without the burden of the pedant's influence.

When I went to visit Owen the second or third or eighth time, he said, "I love you," a statement filled with thought or non-thought which, moments later, made me want to throw myself in front of a subway train, an interestingly extreme response to his relatively innocuous declaration, a response which made me more interested in him. Let's think now: the blunt nail, the blunt ring, foot crippled by arthritis, red sheets. Was there blood on the sheets? My eyes play tricks on memory.

Entering his mouth with my tongue was like entering the atmosphere of another age, his breath an asphyxiating growth to which were attached musty books inscribed in now-fading India ink; costumes he had saved from past productions; framed watercolors by former lovers (the artists Charles Sebree and St. Clair Christmas); a plethora of clothes and mementos stiff with the dry rot of age, or curling in a dim sun obscured by gray clouds, as if left to the elements. Entering his mouth was like entering his apartment on 51st Street on autumn afternoons where one might find the poet Derek Walcott in a black turtleneck, his dark hair and light eyes already brilliant with future success and the reverence of his European colleagues; or the actress Ruby Dee, who suffocated any and all public space with her air of beleaguered "goodness"; or the writer Ed Bullins, whose plays Owen had staged at Howard and whom Owen categorized as a "nigger" because he envied Bullins's self-absorption-induced success.

The reflection and isolation required to produce writing, good, bad, or indifferent, had never been as important to Owen as being liked. "I like you," he said, his breath shouting up into my face like the stale air drummed up by a million dull moths. Visiting him in that apartment, I saw an interesting decorating principle at work— loneliness was at its core; and it was overlaid with the style of the '30s, which was more Negro than black.

His apartment was also filled with illness, sexual despair, a propensity to be rhetorical, a talent to amuse. In photographs taken during his adolescence, the image he presented to the world was one of a slightly small-shouldered confidence—shirts with starched collars and a thin, vulnerable neck. When I looked at these photographs, carefully preserved and cherished in his family photo albums, I always saw his loneliness in the position of his neck. Later, after he began stacking illness up around him, he supported his largish head with the help of his right hand. In those later photographs, that hand blocks our view of his neck.

Besides his thin neck, he had small feet and distended hips, one of which was artificial. He also had a fondness for thinly sliced cheese, weighty silver jewelry, and a vague dislike of women, at least sexually. He competed with women sexually for what he desired: men—one of which he did not consider himself to be. Women were interesting to him as performers, since they could project in any of the plays he could direct what he could project with me only in the dark: his desire to be overcome by a force bigger than his "personality." There was his personality, there were the dust motes, and there I was, his one good leg wrapped around my waist, his trousers pulled down to his knees, perhaps thinking (he did not say): *And after this beloved, another and another.* But he did not say that; I'm imagining that for him now, since this is my story, finally, or, rather, a story I fight to own, since it is not independent of any and all of the people I have known, their shared gestures of intimacy or remorse, his leg wrapped around my waist as the dust motes circled my eyes, which reflected the gravity that pulled his face down around his pillow.

I have always hated to observe things, always, because to observe anything has meant I will remember it, and I have only wanted to experience Fidelity, Love, and Loss, in order to leave them all behind, and move on to the next experience. For some of us, each "fresh wave of consciousness is poison," as Marianne Moore wrote, and I knew, as I began to remove my shoes and socks in Owen's presence and before his shuttered eyes—it was dark whenever we were together sexually; he preferred the lights off, and before the lights were turned out, he shuttered his eyes—that I needed him as much as he needed me, which was my first experience of love—and the will I have always applied to avoiding it.

Sometimes, I heard the sound of birds on his terrace as our tongues became softer and softer toward each other in the experience of pleasure, as student and teacher, child and adult, man and woman—whatever. The birds, I imagined, were pigeons, steel gray like the night sky and the city itself, onto which his apartment door opened.

His apartment was a way station for personal mythologizing; in it, the personal history of celebrities was evoked. He said to me: "Chile, Mrs. Patrick Campbell always had the last word in her plays. She was appearing in Ibsen's *Ghosts*. In *Ghosts*, the son has the last word. On opening night, people waited expectantly to see what Mrs. Campbell would do. The curtain was going down. Her son in the play says his last line: 'Give me the sun, mother, the sun.' The curtain was almost down. Mrs. Campbell said, 'No.'"

He said: "Chile, I met Billie Holiday through my boyfriend, Karl Priebe, in the '40s. She was appearing in a club in New York, on 52nd Street. I came up from Washington to see Karl. He was working, and he suggested I come along to meet her. Chile, she was in this awful dressing room, smaller than my small bathroom. She called me 'Teach.' Her dress was hiked up around her waist. She was fanning her pussy with a fan. She said, looking straight at me, fanning her pussy, 'Teach, it's so goddamn hot in here.'"

Owen said: "Chile, Alain Locke was in love with Langston all those years, so long, the poor thing broke—he lost his mind. Alain was very close to his mother, you know. Anyway, Alain's mother finally died. But he couldn't bear to be separated from her. So he had her all dressed up and propped up in a chair. Then he had all the colored queens come over to take tea with his dead mother. He'd lead a queen over to where she sat, imperious, in her pearls, fortified by her son's filial devotion. 'Mother,' he'd say, 'you remember Owen,' and so on."

The point is, I wanted to be as close to all this as possible—the glamour of creation—in order to write it down. Owen, on the other hand, preferred literary society to writing. In order to be closely associated with what he admired, he told stories about the great he had known marginally; if he could not be a great writer, he would have access to greatness. The men he had known as a boy, those who comprised the homosexual fraction of the Harlem Renaissance, and who were considered "great," he became friends with. They were like him, at least on the surface: nattering, spinsterish, careful personalities who sacrificed wit on the page for that dry-mouthed abstraction known as the Negro cause.

They were stymied in their desire. Their deepest secrets and desires were codified in poems like Countee Cullen's "To The Three

For Whom The Book," in his collection, *The Black Christ and Other Poems*, published in 1929:

> Once like a lady
> In a silken dress,
> The serpent might eddy
> Through the wilderness,
> Billow and glow
> And undulate
> In a rustling flow
> Of sinuous hate.
> Now dull-eyed and leaden,
> Of having lost
> His Eden
> He pays the cost. . . .
> But you three rare
> Friends whom I love. . . .
> A book to you three
> Who have not bent
> The idolatrous knee. . .

Owen said: "Chile, one of the people Countee dedicated that poem to was his boyfriend, Harold Jackman, right after Countee decided he had to go straight and get married. I heard Harold's sister, Ivy, burned all those fabulous letters Countee sent."

The fags Owen had grown up admiring did not have direct access to their emotional lives. They built complete narratives around love they could not reciprocate unless that love was brief, experienced while on sabbatical or waylaid in a port in Naples. Instead of having relationships, they decorated their hearts and apartments in fabulous '30s style, a style that was a terrible joke on a world they assumed could take what they had to offer if they presented it in its correct form. The result: their "correct" sartorial sense—the bow ties and tweed suits of the English schoolmaster. They were never "dirty." They were never "incorrect." They kept their fingernails blunt. Their ability to suck up the dust motes of disturbance, anger, and bad feeling was admirable. Patrick O'Connor, the poet who was for a time Owen's roommate in Washington, D.C. in the early '50s, said to me once: "I loved being taught upperclass manners by a black person." They looked with some disdain on the personal hygiene of white faggots, whom they considered the worst thing imaginable, "nasty," although they coveted their "allure." Because of Owen's eminence as a connoisseur of Negro fags among certain white English and European fags—"Auden was mad for me," he said—he loved recalling the European and English fairies involved in the "arts" who used to call; the fag circuit was very small in the '40s.

Owen arranged a tryst for a black friend whom the actor John Gielgud admired. "And how was it to sleep with one of the greatest living actors of this century?" Owen inquired of his friend the morning after. Owen's friend made a face. He said: "His drawers were shitty."

The women in my family affected respect for him. What the women in my family found difficult to respect was the fact that he was a man, influential in worlds they did not know. Nevertheless, he provoked feelings of jealousy in those women, since he was the first person of substance to claim my attention away from them. One sister in particular (the one most like myself) criticized our relationship beyond recognition. She said, "He's turning my brother into a faggot." I remember how I tried to avoid my sister's scorn by not speaking of Owen, and how often I saw him, how often the dust floated around our joined lips. Early I learned that any personal information offered to powerful women was subject to becoming a narrative outside my control. They could not see me as a boy but only as a teenage girl—as their younger girl-selves, in effect. If I did not submit to their view of me, I would become part of a world they hated. I would become a man, replete with a narrative they could not access. In order to claim me back, they had to chip away at my friendship with Owen. They did so by planting disaster in the air, labeling me a faggot. I had been raised never to contradict women, particularly the women in my own family, even as they tried to kill me with insults as I moved outside their identity. It is only now that I attempt to slip past the identity they established for me, as their younger sister, and into a narrative that, even as I write, rejects my intellection, my control, because I betrayed one of its central characters so long ago: Owen. Back then, I did not say to my mother and sisters: I am already a faggot. I am not a woman. I am not you, but myself, which is what he perhaps loved in his bedroom then, my thin

Death in the Family (1943) by James Van Der Zee (from *The Harlem Book of the Dead*).

chest, the nipples that moved when my bird arms moved. Owen understood my treachery because he knew what deference and fear of women meant; he knew I would give up our friendship for them. He accepted my betrayal as he accepted so much else, holding me in his arms, as I thought: *If I give him up, I will be embraced by the women I know who have yet to claim their lives.* The body alone does not make a woman, but a certain cast of mind does, that cast of mind that creates disaster even as it tries to withstand the disaster it has created. In his room, my lies closed in on me: I had lied by saying I would be with him forever. I lied because he had come to love so late. I knew then that I would come to love late in life as well, when I was no longer able to recognize it as such and had no need to avoid it. I had lied to my sisters and my mother when I told them I would no longer see him. And I caught myself in these lies so that I could disdain all of them for making me lie, and leave myself free to move away from them. That something other than myself I wanted to become had to be a someone who did not come from anywhere where women had the power to displace my love and confusion for men like Owen. I have yet to become that person. Lying there, his lips caked with regret and the need to please, Owen did not say: *He will leave me, as all students do.* He did not say: *You will be many things, a liar foremost, because lying will protect you from yourself.* He did not say: *Look and see what human interaction leads to: lying for convenience.* He clutched my bird arm tighter as I got up to leave. I was nineteen the last time we allowed this intimacy to happen between us. I was nineteen when I left him forever. He had three years to live and we would never speak again. In that moment, I resigned myself to making my way back to the women I presumed loved me and who would not let me go in a metaphysical sense, even though they would go on to other lives, with very little thought to what I had given up for them, for myself: my study of the larger world through this man, to whom I showed no mercy but every tenderness. As I put on my shirt, my naked back turned to him and my first experience of physical love, I was being the good boy I was brought up by women to be, the good boy Owen's sister Lillian had raised him to be, which is to say the kind of boy who would not contradict a woman's position in the world by examining who she was and asking himself what that might mean to him. Lillian's ghost hovered in the best poem Owen was to write, a poem that accompanied a book of photographs by James Van Der Zee called *The Harlem Book of the Dead.* It is comprised of images taken at funeral parlors and at mourners' homes; they are photographs of the living courting the dead. Owen's poem is five lines long. In it, he says:

> We grew so lonely knowing one another
> Please was our only vocabulary now and again
> Will you be with me please
> A word with a vegetable sound
> Please

The photograph Owen's poem accompanied showed two coffins, which held a brother and sister. The poem was spoken from the mouth of the dead woman.

DANNY TISDALE

The Black Museum

Kodak Advertisement, 1970s, 1990.
Offset printing on cardboard, 42 x 42 in.
p. 161

Black Panther Jacket, 1968, 1990.
Leather, size medium.
p. 162

Dashiki, 1969, 1990.
Cotton, size large.
p. 163

Afro Hair (Actual), Different Types, 1960s, 1990.
Actual Afro hair, plastic container, and numbers, 7 $\frac{1}{2}$ x 9 in.
p. 164 (top)

Dax, Slick-Black and Nu Nile Hair Oil (Pomade), 1960s, 1990.
Metal and glass, 2 $\frac{1}{2}$ x 3 $\frac{1}{2}$, 3 x 1 $\frac{7}{8}$, 2 $\frac{1}{2}$ x 1 $\frac{7}{8}$ in.
p. 164 (bottom)

Crack Cocaine, 1990s, 1993–94.
Cocaine, plastic, 9 x 12 x 15 in.
p. 165 (top)

African-American Potato Chips, 1990s, 1993–94.
Paper and potatoes, 20 x 29 $\frac{1}{4}$ x 9 in.
p. 165 (bottom)

Newport Advertisement with Graffiti, 1994.
Tin and paint, 18 x 24 in.
p. 166

Album covers, 1990.
Cardboard and vinyl, approximately 42 x 42 in.
p. 167

Danny, The Last African-American, 2194 (back view), 1994.
(Performance view: 80 Mercer Street, New York.)
p. 168

163

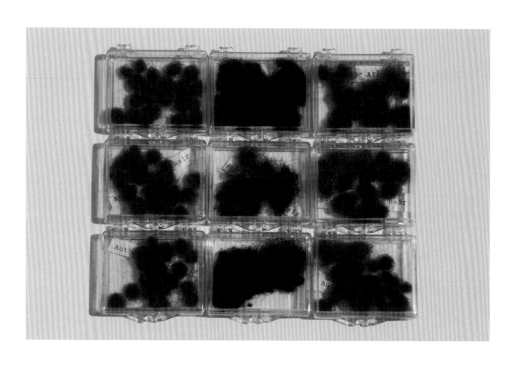

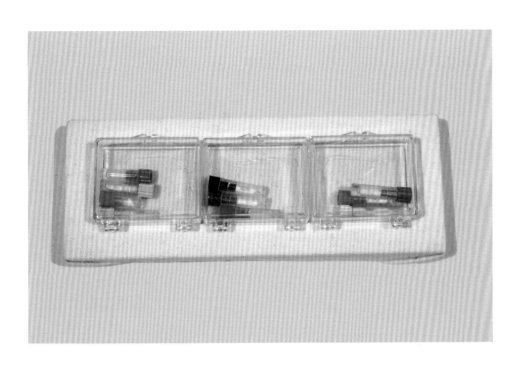

The Last African-American, "Danny"
Age, 34 years. Height, 5 feet 11 inches.
Weight 170 pounds. Brought from Compton,
California, United States of America,
Anthropological Free Agent
By appointment only

The mimicry of museological practices of cataloguing and preservation, display and presentation, provides one of a range of rhetorical frameworks upon which Danny Tisdale hangs his practice of social critique. In *The Black Museum*, the spotlight falls on consumer goods, running the gamut from clothing to foodstuffs to cosmetics to malt liquor and cigarette brands specifically aimed at the African-American market. Clothing that has acquired particular significance—such as the black leather jacket that became almost a uniform for the Black Panther Party, and the dashiki which indicates allegiance to Pan-Africanist ideals—are displayed side by side. The packaged consumer goods resonate on various levels: while some subtly perpetuate racial and ethnic stereotypes, others, such as skin-lightening creams, appeal to assimilative urges. Others, including some images found on 1970s album covers, are symbolic of affirmative currents and images in African-American society.

Tisdale includes his own physical body in these presentations, going so far as to place himself on a pedestal as a specimen for future anthropological study. By displaying himself, Tisdale wields that double-edged sword of social critique and self-promotion: while he invokes the slave auction block on one hand, he also presents himself as heir to that tradition of showmanship that can be found in Charles Willson Peale's painting *The Artist in His Museum* (1822), in which the image of Peale drawing back a curtain far overshadows the gallery of paintings he is revealing; he thus situates himself, as artist, at the focal point between the viewer and the pictures displayed.

—Jackie McAllister

Artaud's True Family, Glimpsed at Beaubourg

"10 years   the language is gone
what's taken its place
this thundering atmosphere
         this lightning
facing the atmospheric pressure of beings"

  thus all these nailed pages,
measled women   targeted hands
spikes & cabinets
which batter the language about the page

"Anyway, Antonin Artaud,
now I'm no longer able to live
a single moment without feeling
in the depths of my being that you
are there
    Paule   30 June
                     1947"

Thévenin's sucked-in cheeks   suspicious & alert gaze
tired on couch tilted   hand grasping neck
in Chinese loafers   left hand across lap
seriously ill [1993]   & denied permission by the Artaud family
to reproduce Artaud's drawings in her book
ce Désespéré qui vous parle
goodbye   Paule Thévenin
you've made a gift for all poets
editing with love   love as editorial act

dedication to the soul of one whose life, ruins,
is, because of you, now a mountain to be climbed

In these portraits
there is ant shrapnel in the faces
aboriginal x-ray organs
the face a living tumulus
living nest of white ants

The sweet lips of Yves Thévenin   24 June 1947

Jany de Ruy's aura of blue hair
explosions in her face   an eye ablaze in her neck
as if the watchers were already present in her face
as if she were already bonneted in rock

Colette Thomas   around August 1947
mouth erased   smudge traceries
hair electrified wire   soft eyes
the sweetness under arched left eyebrow

Henri Pichette   21 November 1947
seems to piston out of void
sailboats race his neck   eyes like grigris
the face as responsible for its own destruction
without title to completion
the human face   slung between
   a tit with thorn for nipple
& traces of derricks   cranes
   the metallurgy of
material encasement

The skull of Colette Allendy
   comes forward to

suck her eyes in
as her hair a huge coiled rope
vanishes into rouge   mouthless spectre,
you are only here now   despectred mouth,
    purse of lips & time

Artaud's own clasped
hands, fingers jutting, rise
    like a single hand
self-portrait December 1946
mummified blind & one-eyed gazing head
floating above this hedgework hand
triple-headed & entire   untitled, around January 1948
Cerberus adrift   head cut loose as 3 heads
how many heads make up our one head?
I was a bee-boy
or are these snails   cuckolding tweezers,
as the heads   fickle to each
    vanish and reappear,
with dearness central to the eyes,
with hair like a shed   as eyes look tombeyond
    asleep beheaded head
with hair like angry seaweed

Jacques Prevel   26 April 1947
eyes & nose a twisted
    sardonic knot
over tense valentine lips

Roger Blin's brain ascends through
    his uprising hair
22 November 1946
head of rock   law of the jaw of man

Coffins wheel about Paule Thévenin's
   reflective stare
24 May 1947   coffins or hinges
"Paule aux ferrets"   ferrets or rivetings,
the irons that break and crackle about what we hear
the curling beauty of her face
   with curling hair
shot through with lightning
totemic inserts
a crocodile races away
something else yet to be defined
   is about to attach itself
to her face.

—28 September 1994

Interpretations

The following conversation between composer/conductor Pierre Boulez, Salzburg Festival director Gerard Mortier, and conductor/pianist Julian Reynolds took place in Amsterdam on October 4, 1995, the day that Boulez's production of Schoenberg's Moses and Aaron *(coproduced by German director Peter Stein) premiered at the Netherlands Opera.*

JULIAN REYNOLDS   In 1963, Mr. Boulez, you were invited to conduct the Paris Opera's production of Alban Berg's *Wozzeck*: you shocked the Parisian music world by demanding thirty-five orchestra rehearsals, which was an unheard-of request at that time, and you triggered a revolution in the attitudes toward music theater and the quality of performance.

Mr. Mortier, when you began as director of the Théâtre Royal de la Monnaie in Brussels in 1981, you also demanded a new level of preparation in opera performance. Now many theaters and institutions follow the basic guidelines that the two of you set down. Having created this new standard, are you satisfied or is further revolution required?

PIERRE BOULEZ   In that performance of *Wozzeck* in '63, I was very careful—the chosen number of rehearsals was clearly specified in the contract—because the musicians had never played anything like that music before. Also, in opera, you have to perfect not only the music, but the relationship between the singers, who are also actors, and the music. If as the music director of a production you do not get involved with the staging, and with the problems of the staging, then you will never, never have a proper performance. Of course, the constraints I like to work with are difficult to meet, but as much as possible, you have to present something decent. I have always fought and I am still fighting for this quality and if the conditions are not there, I will not accept a job. It is as simple as that.

The advantage of Bayreuth, for instance, where I started the *Ring* cycle with Patrice Chéreaux in 1976, is that we had five years to improve it. The first year, a lot of the ideas were there, but their realization still had to be perfected, on stage as well as in the orchestra pit. As time went by, we adapted to each other. By the second year, we knew we were on a track that was taking us somewhere. The third and fourth years, we made great improvements. The fifth year, we really achieved something. You cannot produce *The Ring* in just one go and be satisfied with it. It is a very difficult piece with a long range. You cannot absorb all that heavy German food in a couple of minutes.

GERARD MORTIER

That performance of *The Ring* was something so special that after twenty years I still see it as a classical mother of interpretation. But we should be careful never to think that the interpretation is the only truth about the work. A theatrical interpretation always takes place within an aesthetic and it reflects the trends and concerns of a certain time. It is good to work on it, and it should be the best you can do, but you must always be aware that after ten years you may want to do it again, because your view of the work may have changed again. It is only valid for a limited time and it is not correct to say that one production is more true than another. It is only another experience.

PIERRE BOULEZ

You must keep changing organically. When I am asked if I listen to my recordings, I say no. I don't want to listen to them because I don't want to imitate myself. I don't want to see my photograph of a score from twenty years ago; I want to go back to the score and take another picture. My ongoing experience of conducting has changed the view I have of scores, as has my continuing experience as a composer. For me, the two things are completely tied together.

JULIAN
REYNOLDS

Are you ever inspired or affected by what you see on stage when you're conducting? Does it change your view of a work?

PIERRE
BOULEZ

I try to be part of it. In *Moses and Aaron*, for example, there is the concert performance, and there is also the theatrical performance. Of course, you try to bring the drama into the music, but when people are actually moving on the stage and inhabiting the characters, you must be more flexible and adaptable musically—livelier in a way. Imagine, for instance, when the chorus is spread out across the stage—it is much more difficult to draw them together and stop them from losing my track or their track. Sometimes the story is so violent, musically and on stage, that I have to reflect and encourage that mood of speed and violence, that *hard* music. Other times, when two protagonists are having a dialogue, I try, on the contrary, not to bother them at all. You have two possible attitudes: Either you drive people or you accompany them. Of course, an opera like *Wozzeck*, with all its divisions and complex rhythms, is technically less easy than Mozart, but you have to adapt.

I remember the first time I ever heard *Wozzeck* performed in concert in Paris in 1949 or '50, I saw Marie, after she had supposedly died on stage, put her fur coat back on and sit down at the front of the audience. It was simply ridiculous. It was awful. That was the first performance of *Wozzeck* I ever saw and I will never forget it.

JULIAN
REYNOLDS

Over the last years, you have been very instrumental in developing the new technology of music, as well as the new technology of communication. Are there are any real artistic merits to the recording industry or is it simply an archive?

PIERRE
BOULEZ

Recordings document the performances of a time. As Gerard just said, theater ages very quickly, but it's like film: if a film is fundamentally good—like the films of Eisenstein—it doesn't matter that it is dependent on its time. Recordings also help the dissemination of culture. It is always said that opera is for the elite, but the more you create documents of this kind, the more you will make people aware of what culture can be and they will demand much more. They will not be satisfied with mediocre performances by people who arrange concerts between cups of tea.

The danger is that people will mistake the document, the recording, for the score. They think that the realization of the opera they are hearing is the *only* realization. Most people cannot read a score, so they believe that what they hear *is* the score. That is their misunderstanding. The score is something much more flexible. When people hear contemporary performances of Beethoven, they often say, "That will never be as good as Furtwängler." Of course Furtwängler was a great conductor of Beethoven. But he had the ideas of his time, and he saw the scores of Beethoven's works through his own prism. It was Beethoven through a prism, however coherent or logical.

GERARD MORTIER   It is beautiful to see what a pyramid looks like in a photograph. I have never been to Egypt, but at least I have a photograph. But it would be completely stupid to say that that photograph *is* a pyramid. You must stand in front of the pyramid to really understand it.

PIERRE BOULEZ   Proust says a marvelous thing about photographs. He says that when we look at old photographs, it is impossible for us to distinguish between the count and the butcher, because we cannot recognize the things that make them different—the tie or the way of buttoning a jacket. These distinctions in our own society are very obvious to us. But people fifty years from now will confuse the artist and the butcher in our photographs. Look at people in the summer on the beach. They are all in swimming trunks: Where is the butcher? Where is the artist?

JULIAN REYNOLDS   Where do you think opera is heading? Should we perpetuate the system and institutions that we now have?

GERARD MORTIER   The way things are now working out is very disturbing to me. There has been a great revival of the opera of the post–Second World War period. The traditional repertoire is getting old and much of it now seems boring, so we look for and sometimes rediscover the most frightful forgotten pieces. The directors of opera houses are all small princes—in the long tradition of princes who commissioned operas. This has its good sides and its very bad sides and in such a great project as *Moses and Aaron*, it's very important to make coalitions between princes which we can exploit. What Pierre has done with *Moses* is beautiful because he has done it in homage to a work that deserves to be revived.

I think that opera as an art form is an ironic art. Our understanding is completely bound to the spirit of our modern times. I believe that there will be a time when we won't want to write any more operas. And at some point in the future, when people look back and see how we performed our tragedies and comedies, they will consider them as outdated as yesterday's video game.

PIERRE BOULEZ

The conditions for continuing the growth of opera are not easy to find, primarily because it now requires so much work to produce. I fought—and I failed, I must say—at the Bastille in Paris to create a flexible hall, a Salle Modulaire, which would be mobile and which could give us the architectural conditions to experience opera without the heavy machinery of old opera houses, and would encourage new forms through the flexibility of the space.

GERARD MORTIER

One of the greatest problems for composers today is that they have to compose pieces for opera houses that were built in the nineteenth century. The disaster is that we never built an opera house for composers of the twentieth century. This is one of the great mistakes of contemporary French culture.

JULIAN REYNOLDS

As Kenneth Clark said, when they stopped building cathedrals, they started building opera houses. Now they have also stopped building opera houses.

PIERRE BOULEZ

Absolutely. At the La Villette cultural center in Paris, we were able to build a concert hall which is mobile. It was inaugurated in January 1995, and we have seen in only one season how necessary it was to build it, because it simplifies life. We don't fight against the architecture, the architecture works with us. In today's music, we have to relate groups of performers in new ways. If we cannot do that, we will not be able to incite young people to come to the opera.

Periform

A colloquium on form?*
Certainly!
To tackle such a subject without fear is to assume that one is fully in command of "the rest." What imprudence, to undertake such a risky investigation!

Is content less important to discuss?

For the time being, in any case, no colloquium on content is planned ("to be discussed . . . ").

So here we are, on a highly educational cruise, riding the raft of form and well provisioned with sentences, speeches, and words.

The truth is that I don't feel especially inclined to pay exorbitant tribute to the many problems that besiege us. I feel no temptation to trace things back to the time of the Flood. No demon has come to whisper provisional or definitive justifications in my ear. If demon there be, it finds me more inclined to wander at will.

I will quote myself, as a frontispiece: "Dreaming your revolution is no less essential than making it."

Without denying the truth of this motto, I am allowing myself the freedom not to dream up any revolution here, and I count on others to provide me with any number of solid, robust, and

---

* Paper read to a colloquium on "Form in Contemporary Music" held in Darmstadt in 1965.

substantial arguments, so that I may speak, as it were, a versatile, humorous, or arabesque language.

So much for opening remarks!

Form: or the word, Jarry might have said . . .

Or another quotation, Webern in reference to Hölderlin: To live is to defend a form. I alone am responsible for what I deduce from this remark, for I shall begin with the converse: a form is a defense of life. Or more egocentrically, a form is a defense of one's own life.

I could easily conjugate musical fate—or any other fate: let's not be exclusive!—according to the following ritual:

I		form.
You	trans	form.
He	de	forms.

The root is, dare I say, proteiform:

> formal
> formalism
> formation
> information
> informal
> formula
> unformulated
> formulary
> formulation
> forming, etc.
> And don't forget:
> formidable!

(I don't exclude deception on principle.)

I recall that an aesthete more clever than he was shrewd once confided or confessed (among the many confidences and innumerable confessions he made) his true predilections. What he said in substance, while playing on his substantives, was this: "I prefer the forms of life to the life of forms."

I could fuse Hölderlin and Cocteau together by saying: "Rather than defend one's life in forms, I prefer to defend the forms of life." What a ringing manifesto! Enough to keep generations of luminous humanists busy.

We are not, alas, at a colloquium on humanism. I must therefore forgo the pleasure of discussing the many implications of this aphorism. (On the subject of humanism, many ideologues, it seems to me, use this key word in contrast to formalism. But they use it in the same way other people use the weather to introduce a joke.)

Form: this word, this master-word and word of the master, puzzles me.

The more one tries to grasp its meaning, the more elusive it becomes. The more one tries to pin it down historically, the more it loses reality.

The less one talks about it, the more it pricks up its ears. The more one argues about it, the less one succeeds in making oneself understood.

There are questions that one is compelled to ask oneself over and over, in an endless echo, until the echo itself becomes incongruous.

What is form?

What is f...?

What is ...?

What ...?

Wh ...?

? (I won't discuss the irreverent form of the echo.)

Is the virgin forest a form?

No doubt . . .

Then imagination is also a form.

Is that enough to convince anyone?

I don't think so. But the farther I go, the less I trust the virtues of conviction: that widow holds little interest for me.

I adopt the Rimbaud/Infernal method:

"One night, I sat Form (with a capital F, of course) down on my lap. (Why not? There's nothing indecent in that!)—And I found her bitter (surely the same thing has happened to many people, even those who never dared to sit Form on their laps...)—And I insulted her (I would bet that the number of people who have engaged in such an expression of contempt is far smaller.)"

I could continue my parody of this poem, but then it would become a scholastic exercise—dead form!

Spring or autumn, it would bring us only "the idiot's frightful laugh."

Let us turn forever
            around
the tallest tower.

Form:

Is it a gesture, an accident? A series of gestures, a series of accidents?

Is it chance encountered?

Is it a discipline?

Is it a truth to discover or reinvent?

Is it a conception? A will?

Is it a pattern inherited through a maze?

Is it an organized labyrinth?

Is it a revelation?
            An illumination?
                        A shock?

Is it doubt?

Is it trial-and-error?

Is it the mystery that is constantly reforming itself around the evidence?

Is it . . . a black sun?

Questions about questions . . .

Old alchemy, I have found your traces; and I am not satisfied.

For better or for worse, patterns have lost their reality. We must accommodate ourselves to this irremediable void and fill it instead with . . . what? Is that not precisely the question?

Form, that pretty philosopher's stone, the search for which amuses well-behaved, serious, grown-up children: will they find it or won't they?

I juxtapose, I shock: is this a form in embryo?

Can I stick to what has happened, or must I include what is foreseen?

To what extent can I mislead the decipherer of dreams? Must I provide the keys of comprehension? Or can I wall myself up in my imaginary fortress?

"How easy it is to write, how difficult to compose."

No exclamation point. This might be a chapter title, objective. In its ultimate definition, form would probably play a role of spectral analysis—entirely spectral, even!

Who shall express the toil of transmutation, the tortures of formal transubstantiation? Some day if I feel myself better equipped for describing ghosts . . .

Can the unexpected proximity of an umbrella, a sewing machine, and a dissecting table by itself create a form? An absurd question, the need for which may not be absolutely clear, but the pertinence of which does not fail at times to make itself felt . . .

Form: *maître-mot*, master-word, I wrote. Or rather, I should have written *maître-mot*, but a slip of the finger made me type *mitre-mot* (prison-word). I could continue to slide down the slope of assonances: *maître-mot, mot de maître; mitre-mot, mot de pître* (clown's word); *piètre-mot* (lame word); *maître-sot* (master-fool) . . . (Sinbad the sailor . . . and other Ulyssean resources!)

L et us restate the *reductio ad absurdum*:
    I do not defend a form, therefore I do not live. True?
    Or: I live, therefore I defend a form. Truer?
More commonly: I live, therefore I do not have to worry about defending a form (unless a political crusade is involved . . .).

Has even a hermit ever said: I worry about defending a form, therefore I do not live?

(If such a hermit existed, it would be imperative to find him at all costs and bring him immediately to this colloquium. He would be capable of providing us with interesting new information. But he might contemplate us with silent commiseration and then leave without explaining himself, leaving us hungry for knowledge. And we would be reduced more than ever to patiently piling umbrellas and sewing machines onto dissecting tables!)

In principle, I start by living. At least I try to, as much as I can. (Is it as easy as people think and say it is?) I live, that much is sure; but I am keen to acquire knowledge. What is a human being without knowledge? He is no different from an animal . . . So, long live study!

So here I am, with my small amount of baggage, when suddenly, in order to be original, I get rid of it: the best teachers always urge this quite vigorously. How could I dare not to follow their advice on this most important point!

Thus I find myself staggering along in the present.

How am I going to dominate events? Reclaim my little piece of baggage? Or deliberately allow my fever to take over, and rejoice in drawing diagrams of my creative energy? The problem of problems.

How should I form myself, how should I formulate myself? Operating on myself, I would have to freeze lightning! (The comparison, bold as it is, is not entirely out of place.)

Alchemy of language, which is not yet done deceiving us . . .

Rereading what I wrote some time ago, I find my words quite serious, as the occasion warranted.

Some of those words transcribed:*

Form and content are identical in nature, subject to the same analysis. Content derives its reality from its structure, and what one calls form is the structuring of local structures, which constitute the content.

(These words are not mine, moreover, but those of an eminent anthropologist, Lévi-Strauss; I simply adapted them for my purpose.)

Is this the inexpressible, noted? Is this whirling confusion, nailed down?

It was certainly a study . . .

I continue my rereading and discover certain naïvetés which in retrospect I find enchanting. Here is a sample:

To speak of form in general has become quite difficult, because the study of form in general cannot be separated from the study of the particular aspects it exhibits in each work. The best one can do, perhaps, is to isolate a few general organizing principles.

Such extreme prudence is highly laudable, and I still approve of it today. I approve of it more than ever, because I find that there are some subjects that are quite difficult to "colloquiumize."

Nevertheless, I did not fail to dissect certain structural aspects, not having altogether given up hope that, with some effort expended in the dissection, one might reach the land of definition.

The path continued to be arid. At times—frequently—that aridity was disconcerting, in the most literal sense. But in order to reach the Promised Land of definition, through what deserts would one not pass! At times the Tables of the Law exert a fascination mixed with repulsion, which compels us to be intrepid in our explorations. . . .

---

* The quotations in italics are taken from an earlier text on form.

I also read:

It follows that formal evolution, despite the references, must culminate in an irreversible time, in which the criteria of form are based on a series of relations among differential possibilities. . . . Hence I have no consciousness of form, and my "angle of audition" is not established, until the form has unfolded entirely, a posteriori. . . . I find chance at the conclusion of a logical and coherent deduction.

(This sentence has a certain bizarre quality: I claim the freedom to emphasize this virtue from time to time above all others.)

It will be seen, in the end, that I have tried to define form as a conceptual whole and not as a gesture (if I need a gesture at all, it will find its place in this conceptual whole). At last the contradiction between "thought form" and "experienced form" seems to me resolved. From the concrete deductions on which form is based within a coherent formal system, it emerges that form can be experienced only through or for thought. Is this not at present an important contradiction to resolve?

Close the book!

Enough of the verb written, transcribed, translated, and frozen in convoluted quotations! Abandon the strict labyrinth of cemented words to stroll at will through architectures improvised in the very moment of uttered speech.

Translated from the French by Arthur Goldhammer

Holding On

Because the dead have no memory
we must always be remembering for them.
You learn now to live under water.
Even if you should grow pale with longing
for sunlight, and sunsets of violet,
you must float with the currents and be of them—

and it is comforting here without the treacherous
shifting temperatures of the earth world.
Some would call it dark
but I say no: here shines
all the light I need. Here everything exists,
only it cannot grow.

When

When the tablecloth and all the settings
fall to the floor, everything in a heap,
the table hard and bare.

When you sprawl headlong, hear a bone break.

When a window shatters and a spider's web
traps your face.

Nowhere

The gurneys positioned like a frieze against the wall,
whey-faced men and women wait for radiation to flood
their bones. The sheet slips back from gnarled feet
and hands lift swollen veins, blue ropes climbing
to nowhere hearts. In these cold corridors,
you learned an alphabet of ending and I stood helpless
as one on shore who witnesses a wreck,
all hands lost before her disbelieving eyes.

Yunus

T he clock on the wall slowly struck nine. So it was three o'clock in the morning. Those archaic, undecipherable, caned Roman numerals were drawn on the darkness. In the narrow, paved courtyard a pair of clogs was trying to prolong the feeling of dawn. If this is an ongoing dream, is it possible not to remember Mother—that tired woman whom the two sleepy oars striking against the white, moonlit stones carried from a storeroom full of pain and cockroaches to a room where beards shook with coughing? The moonlight illuminated an abstract and happy cross-section of the room, a completely isolated cross-section: the marble platform over the sea where the jinns of sleep flew, the red carpet, the pale faces of Uncle Yunus and Grandfather, wriggling like kittens. These were serene, bright faces awash in light. In reality, however, there was no room for such serenity in this huge house with its large and quiet rooms where four very different people breathed the air of the hour of death, an air full of fear and irritation, in this buried universe where the birds of death often touched their hearts softly. In reality, however, I had been aware of this for a long time. I knew the pillars under us were rotting; I knew that one day, along with the old stones, carpets, and broken pieces of mirrors, we would all fall into the damp cellar. I was waiting. We were all waiting. I had reasons for thinking this would happen: Yesterday I heard Mother say to Grandfather: "Isn't it time yet? I will do the pickling tomorrow. Then that will be it! What I'll do won't take more than an hour. Don't tell the others. All I ask is that you bury me under the pomegranate tree. I would freeze up on a mountain. Plus you know I have a weak heart. . . ."

It seems that death is carving into the heart of Uncle Yunus. He says so. He has tried vaguely to show this in late afternoons when he falls into a long and troubled empty mood. In the beginning I did not understand anything. I was a little surprised too. Now I understand. I even seem to feel those wells of emptiness inside me acquiring meaning and taking on their own existence.

Grandfather, I mean Yunus's father, does not seem to think about death. Yet he will be dead in a few days. I'm thinking about leaving the house once all of us are dead.

It's nine-thirty. It should be chillier outside. Cold lilies are drawn on the window. The moon has disappeared. In the stable, the horse starts to neigh. Grandfather wakes up. His beard shakes with a cough. The shaking passes on to Uncle Yunus. They both straighten at the same time. As if trying not to wake me, Grandfather whispers to Uncle Yunus:

"Yunus, son, turn on the light."

Uncle Yunus is still coughing. He gets up, pulling on his long underwear. I shut my eyes just as he reaches to turn on the light. When I open them again that strange zone has been left behind and morning has begun.

So that's it, we have buried death. As if it were never to be. Grandfather is rolling a cigarette. The red carpet, cleaned every day, is almost shiny. On the floor and on the walls there are small kilims with long-horned deer, merry shepherds in boots, and wild flowers. In the courtyard the clogs are no longer strolling sleepily and resound with a wet morning vigor. In the anteroom whistles are screeching from the teapot.

The horse neighs once again.

"Get up, son," says Grandfather, "go feed the horse while the boy is still sleeping!"

Uncle Yunus is coughing.

"I'm sick," he whispers. "Let him feed the horse when he wakes up."

He must be pointing at me. I close my eyes even more tightly. Grandfather gets angry:

"You will never be a man. The same story every morning. Your beard has turned white but look at you!"

Uncle is moaning:

"I said I'm sick. I ache all over. I can't move an inch."

The door is opened roughly. I open my eyes slightly. It is the cat. It comes in clinging to the latch. Following it, Mother. In her hands the tray with the coffee cups on it. Her face looks paler in the light. There are silent lines above her eyebrows. She looks at me. She knows at once that I am not asleep. But she does not say anything. She gives them their coffee. Hesitating, she says:

"I began the pickling. It will be finished by noon."

She is able to perpetuate death, despite the fact that it is morning. She is the only person on earth capable of doing that. She is used to it. She knows she has come to the end. One more thing: Her left hand does not have a little finger. I have never thought about that missing finger before. I have always watched her do things with the other four. But lately I've begun noticing the absence of that little finger. Will this change certain things?

Uncle Yunus utters a deep "ugh." Mother has quietly left the room. The squabble starts again. Grandfather uses the extraordinary stubbornness he has acquired so masterfully over the years that neither Mother nor Uncle knows what to do in face of it. He will push his cap back, scratch his red forehead onto which three white hairs have fallen, put his cherrywood mouthpiece in his mouth—which is lost in his beard—and fix his eyes on one point. I have seen no one in my entire life who fears the Sultan less than he does. He was once a feudal lord. He used to show everyone a tobacco pouch that he had kept from those days.

"Get up, Yunus!" he says again. He wants to irritate Uncle Yunus. Old, sickly Yunus does not know how to answer him back. He likes the horse. However, he also likes the noble ideas he has acquired over the years as well as that pain caused by dismal weather which belongs to him and only him. What can he possibly say, poor sick Yunus? Suddenly he gets overexcited; he cries out with his eyes full of tears, sniffling like a child:

"Let it die! Let our one and only horse die! And let them flay off his skin and throw it to the dogs. Let the crows feed on its dead body, the dogs too! I don't give a damn!"

The cat is scratching at the door outside. Its voice is thin and sharp in the cold. It is as if the cat, too, wants to incite Uncle Yunus.

Grandfather gazes at him with merciless, dirty eyes. His chin is lost in his mouth.

"I'll take off, just like that," Uncle continues, "it doesn't matter where. Then my illness will get worse and I will die and you'll be rid of me."

He dresses quickly. He slams the door behind him as his father watches in amazement. He washes his face at the faucet in the courtyard. Then he opens the main gate and leaves. The sound of Mother's clogs stops for a moment, then starts again. She rushes into the room. "Where did he go?" she asks. Grandfather does not answer. All he does is prod me and say with a stiff look on his face: "He forgot his cane. Catch up with him and give it to him." I take the cane. I dress and hurry out. Mother gives me two slices of bread with cheese. In the stable the horse groans like an old bandit dying in the afternoon.

I go out into the street. A gleaming cold. My foot hits something soft. It is the dead body of a bird. These small birds, they cannot survive any more. I throw its light body over our neighbor's wall. I pass stores with low ceilings and narrow shutters and quiet houses in the Armenian style. I know where to look for Uncle. I follow the long wall into whose holes wish-stones have been inserted. An odd minaret with an umbrella, its top demolished. Next to it, the ruins of a small mosque. An old oak tree is multiplying its leafless branches in the dark. I go into the ruins. I find Uncle in a small room which somehow or other has not been demolished. The ceiling is covered with soot and there is only an old mat on the floor. On the walls are shelves, books, and ancient musical instruments. In the corner, under a patched cloak, lies a hermit with a red beard. The jinns of sleep—or perhaps the wind—play in his beard. Uncle Yunus is reading a thick old book, the one he always reads. Stories told by a musical instrument—in candlelight, murmuring. I place his cane in a corner, sit, and start to watch him.

After some time, a strange game starts. It is hard to believe it is happening, in the darkness and silence. Uncle Yunus is reading his book, muttering to himself, and is, at the same time, folding into himself. He is being folded and then rolled up like a piece of paper or a cardboard pipe. At first I am terrified. I try hard not to scream. Then suddenly I understand what is happening. Uncle is concentrating and is widening the emptiness around him which resembles death. I feel that he understands things which no one else can and that he is being buried. He is folded into eternity; his body, his eyes are getting smaller and smaller. He is a book that is being closed, never to be opened again.

The candle melts away. It burns to the very end.

For some time I stand there, dumbfounded. When I recover my senses I see that morning light is coming in quietly through the door. I am almost frozen. I get up. I walk toward the corner where the book and the desk remain invisible in the dark. I bend over Uncle and see that his eyes are frozen in an offended stare, his white beard is no longer trembling and his motionless body lies in a tired curl. I want to take him respectfully by the arm and make him get up—as if he were still alive. He is as light as the body of a dead bird, yet big. I let him fall back into his comfortable curl. I am still holding the cane. The hermit is sleeping. The sunlight is about to hit his red beard. Of the four of us Uncle Yunus was the first to go. Who is next, Mother?

I go out. The courtyard of the mosque is in ruins; it is quiet— no one around but a rooster. It bends over the pool which is like a huge mirror somehow forgotten under the naked branches of the oak tree. The rooster shakes his golden feathers. It crows with a vigor that does not befit this pale, wretched atmosphere. The morning is pierced.

Translated from the Turkish by Aysenur Güvenir

Belle Starr

Belle, Wake up
Her cheek resting on the icy pond.

Shadow of a thug turkey-shot her
in the back, neck and breast
Colt tore through her face

Her last bath
in turpentine and crimson cinnamon.
Pallbearers dangle six-shooters.

Cornbread in the coffin
Wake up, Belle

•

On the other side the bread was et
her outlaw in-laws provanded.
A smile welds those wire lips
under wired lids—black
beaded eyes, a sky
on ceiling tacked, another world.
Only it is opposite,
so when she dies here, she finds her hope,
hemp-rope holding all in place
with peckish ravens darting back and forth.

•

Father was an innkeeper. We called him
Judge for his sternness and popularity.

(He locked her in
his closet, to keep her
his Confederate virago)

a wingbeat

the haunts the hurts, ball and chain

In dream you crackle like ice over earth
like lust against the plains.

•

As a child, to harbor a secret
lands you in bondage;
then, as a woman, outlaws
harbor in your heart and land

Belle a born uglee

eyes evolved not
because of mind's need to see—
but neurons must pre-exist
with a light sensitivitee

•

Cherokee sun is she

•

Down Dallas way she's
The Bandit Queen,
Queen of the Outlaws,
Long velvet train
Riding her stallion Black Venus
Down the main

Faro table, whiskey up and those
Jolly lads, southern night riders

While Jim was out, a scout
For the next crime scene

Nesters, squatters, shooters
Who'd disarm or arrest her?

Who'd undress her?
A forty-five under her skirt.

•

Word has it the Tumbleweed Wagon rolls
and gangs travel, wheat in the wind.
The iron-rimmed wheel prison
wields fear from afar where humans
like hounds armed to the teeth
are shackled in irons and washing
the dishes and fighting
fires that burn through the prairies.

When Belle and Sam Starr were apprehended
on a horse-stealing charge, she tossed out
the blankets, the pots and the pork,
the stove, and the fork. So the marshal tossed
Belle on the cold metal floor with rebuke.

That year, she fixed 'em a grand supper of rattlesnake stew.
And coffee like glue.

Rolled on the floor as they puked.

Yes, The Petticoat of the Plains, dare-may-care. She rolled
on the floor as they puked. Thus, outlaws sought her advice.

•

She, their Guiding Spirit, gave chase
In black invisible

Wound in a buckskin
Of rattlesnake rattlers

Up north the Hi-Early Mountains
Far west a cranberry sunset
The earth on Cherokee Nation

Only approach to her cabin
Was through a narrow canyon

Fortlike with fine furniture
Famed for its Hawkins's Portable Grand,
And its Belle Starr Creek

She washed her feet and raised
Her girl, Pearl, to be a lady

•

Coarser variations of air produce sound

Stillwater Penitentiary

Released on bond and a shopping spree

Each husband shot, replaced

She could read the wanted posters
on each face

Their obituaries
she could read

•

With the grace of a cat
the Colt left his holster

Velvet sky
Moon on high
Last star seen

BRIGID BERLIN

The Cock Book

Cover of *The Cock Book (Topical Bible)*, 1968–73.
Leather with gold embossment, approximately 9 x 7 x 3 in.
p. 201

Page by Brigid Berlin.
Collage with photograph and receipt.
p. 202

Page possibly by a waitress from Max's Kansas City, New York.
Collage with aluminum foil.
p. 203

Page by Brigid Berlin.
Collage with sponge.
p. 204

Page by Brigid Berlin.
Spray-paint silhouette of hypodermic needle.
p. 205

Page possibly by Andy Warhol.
Collage with rubber.
p. 206

Hungarian Packing House collage by Brigid Berlin.
Photographic collage.
p. 207

Page by Peter Hujar.
Ink on black-and-white photograph.
p. 208

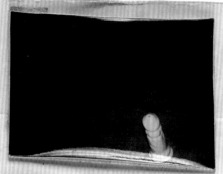

KEEP THIS SLIP. It is your receipt for payment and identifies this transaction in case of any adjustment.

UNITED CAMERA EXCHANGE

STORE

1140 SIXTH AVE. (COR. 44th ST.)
265 MADISON AVE. (COR. 39th ST.)
132 EAST 43rd ST. (COR. LEX. AVE.)
1122 SIXTH AVE. (43 ST.)
1662 BROADWAY (COR. 51st ST.)
25 WEST 44th ST. (ARCADE)

YU 6-1600

NAME *BRSIB BERLIN DECEASED*

ADDRESS *FOTH*

DATE		D & M	SUPPLIES ACCESS.	CAMERA LENSES	FILM	MAG.	AMOUNT REC'D
SALESMAN							

QUAN.	DESCRIPTION	@	AMOUNT
2	C *Flashlight Batteries*		
	for		
	Dildo # 30724		

	AMOUNT		
	SALES TAX	1	67
	TOTAL		

2610-47   All claims and returned goods must be accompanied by this bill.

6①2607   MFD. BY BALTIMORE BUSINESS FORMS, INC., BALTIMORE, MD. 21229

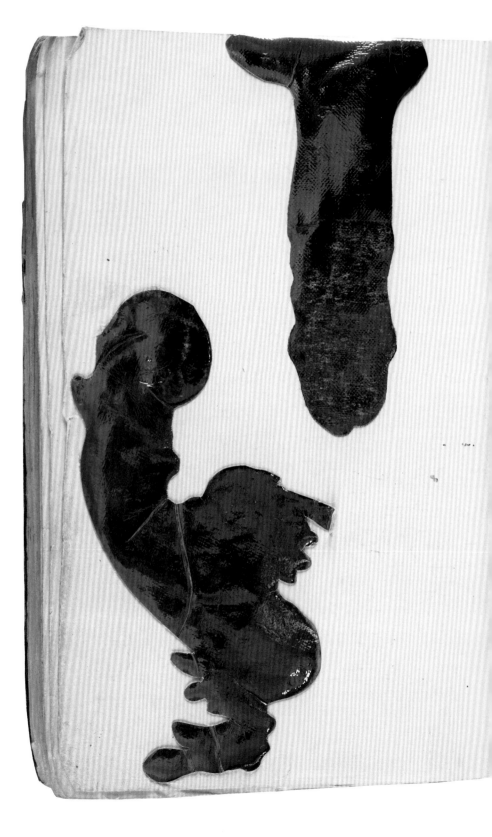

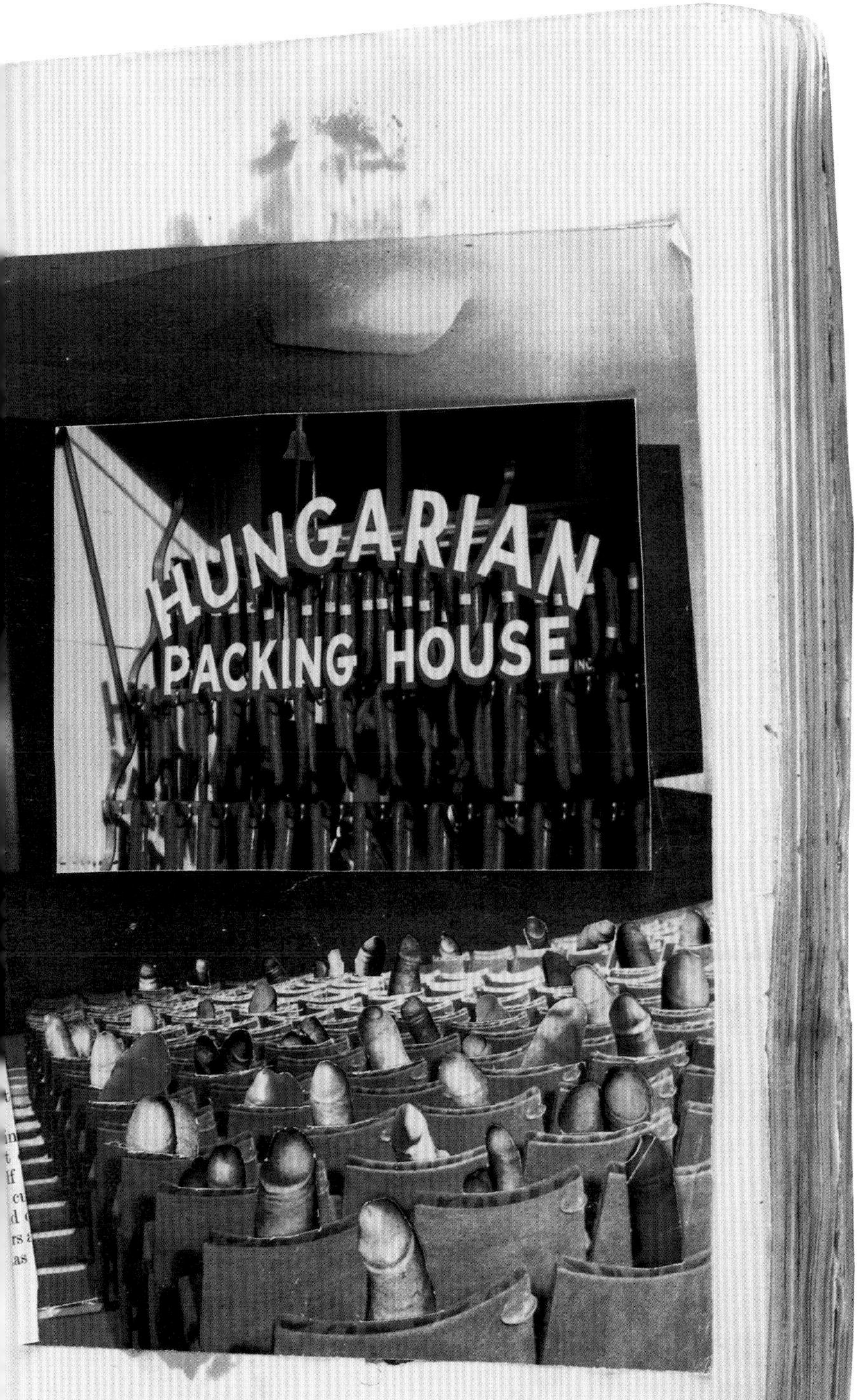
HUNGARIAN
PACKING HOUSE INC.

PETER HUJAR ©
PLEASE CREDIT

At Andy Warhol's Factory, in the back room of Max's Kansas City, or in her apartment in the George Washington Hotel, in Manhattan, Brigid Berlin (known at the time as Brigid Polk) spent much of the 1960s and early '70s recording and transcribing hundreds of hours of monologues, telephone calls, conversations, sexual encounters, and interviews. She also filled dozens of blank books with her own art and with works solicited from almost everyone she knew or met. The Cock Book *was the first of these collections to have a single theme. Berlin was interviewed for* Grand Street *by Vincent Fremont:*

BRIGID BERLIN: At the time, everybody had what we called trip books; we'd keep all our drawings and notes in them. Magic Markers were new then, and everybody would do crazy drawings in everyone else's books. There was a place on 57th Street called Leather Craft where they made beautiful bound books. I used to buy my books there, and I'd have my monogram stamped on the outside.

Then, one day in 1968, I was walking down Broadway and saw this place across from the Strand Bookstore at 12th Street—it's not there anymore—where they had a Bible in the window. It had gilt-edged pages and it was black, with *Topical Bible* stamped on the cover in gold. The spine read *Cruden's Concordance,* whatever that means. And I thought, what the hell kind of Bible is a *Topical Bible?* So I went into the store and the whole book, which was as thick as a real Bible, was actually a blank dummy book. I bought it for ten dollars and I said, this is going to be the first book I've made that will stick with one topic. I walked back up the center of Park Avenue, on the islands, because the streets were filled with snow, carrying my Gucci shopping bag with this Bible in it. I thought about what topic to choose and tried rhyming the word "topical" with several options; "cockical" was the last one I tried. That was how *The Cock Book* started.

The Cock Book Volume Two was another book I found that had *The Story of the Bible* stamped on the cover; that one had the first couple of pages printed and the rest of the pages blank. Then I did *The Tit Book, The Scar Book, The Ear Book,* and *The Tear Book* (I made people cry onto a page and sign it).

Now the books overwhelm me. The Dr. Feelgoods are dead. There's no Andy to trade with.

—Anne Doran

—993–1056 C.E.

I'd Suck Bitter Poison From the Viper's Mouth

I'd suck bitter poison from the viper's mouth
    and live by the basilisk's hole forever,
rather than suffer through evenings with boors,
    fighting for crumbs from their table.

Could Kings Right a People Gone Bad

Could kings right a people gone bad,
   while they themselves are twisted?
How, in the woods, could shadows that bend
   be straight when the trees are crooked?

The Multiple Troubles of Man

The multiple troubles of man,
   my brother, like slander and pain,
amaze you? Consider the heart
   which holds them all
in strangeness, and doesn't break.

Earth to Man

Earth to man
  is a prison forever.

These tidbits, then,
   for fools:

Run where you will.
  Heaven surrounds you.
   Get out if you can.

Translated from the Hebrew by Peter Cole

J. S. DRUCKER

Only the Heads Survive:
Zippo Lighters
from the Vietnam War

*Call it pride, integrity, or just plain cussedness, the Zippo man
believes that when you buy a lighter it should work forever.*

*[A] Zippo, unlike fountain pens, detergents, or cars, is an emotional
object with a high content of personal recollection and interest. Zippo
is not just an article of convenience: it is a memory box . . .*

—Zippo advertising copy

At the army surplus market on the outskirts of Ho Chi Minh
City or in various shops on Dong Khoi Street in the central
District One, tourists, ex-servicemen, collectors of militaria,
and souvenir hunters can buy American G.I.s' Vietnam War–era
Zippo lighters for a few U.S. dollars. Striking in the power of their
symbolism, these icons of American consumer culture—that were
used to light village dwellings as well as cigarettes—present a trace
of the individual soldier within the larger uniform military body.
Some of these lighters are real Zippos that were carried by U.S.
troops in Vietnam; others are counterfeits, engraved recently for
sale to tourists and collectors.

Authentic or not, they present the voice of war, often distorted
by violence witnessed and committed, by the attraction of that violence
as well as by its horror. The Zippos in J. S. Drucker's collection bear
witness to the terrifying sense of power that comes from exposure
to condoned killing (*Let Me Win Your Heart and Mind or I'll Burn Your
God Damn Hut Down*) as well as to the religious despair and political
alienation (*Fuck Communist Fuck De Mocracy Fuck Uncle Ho Fuck Sam
Fuck LBJ Fuck NVA Fuck V.C Fuck 'Santa' Lause Fuck You Too*) which
many servicemen experience. As such they paint a disturbing portrait
of the soldier's inner life.

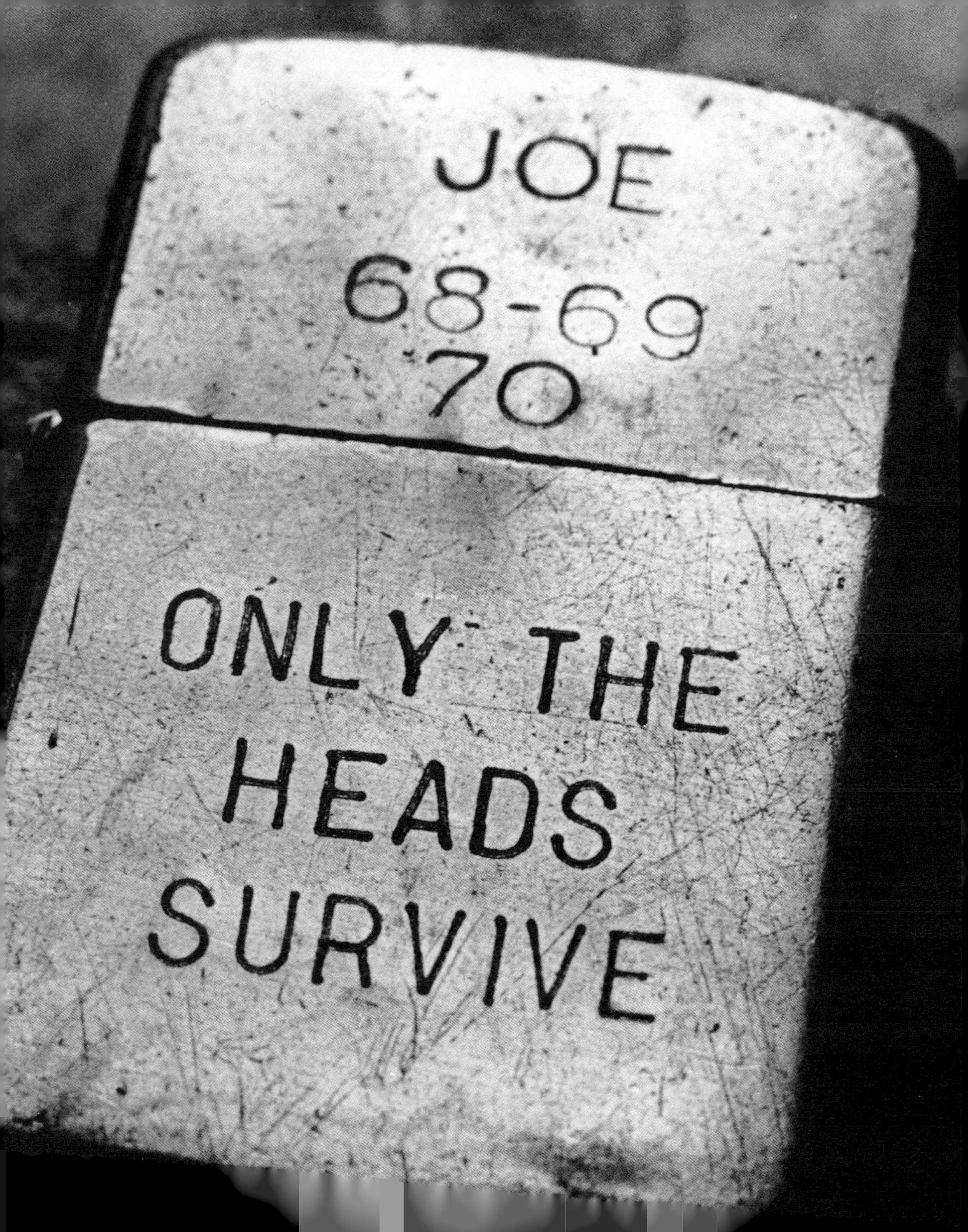
JOE
68-69
70
ONLY THE
HEADS
SURVIVE

FUCK COMMUNIST
FUCK DE MOCRACY
FUCK UNCLE HO
FUCK SAM
FUCK LBJ
FUCK NVA
FUCK V.C
FUCK 'SANTA' LAUSE
FUCK YOU TOO

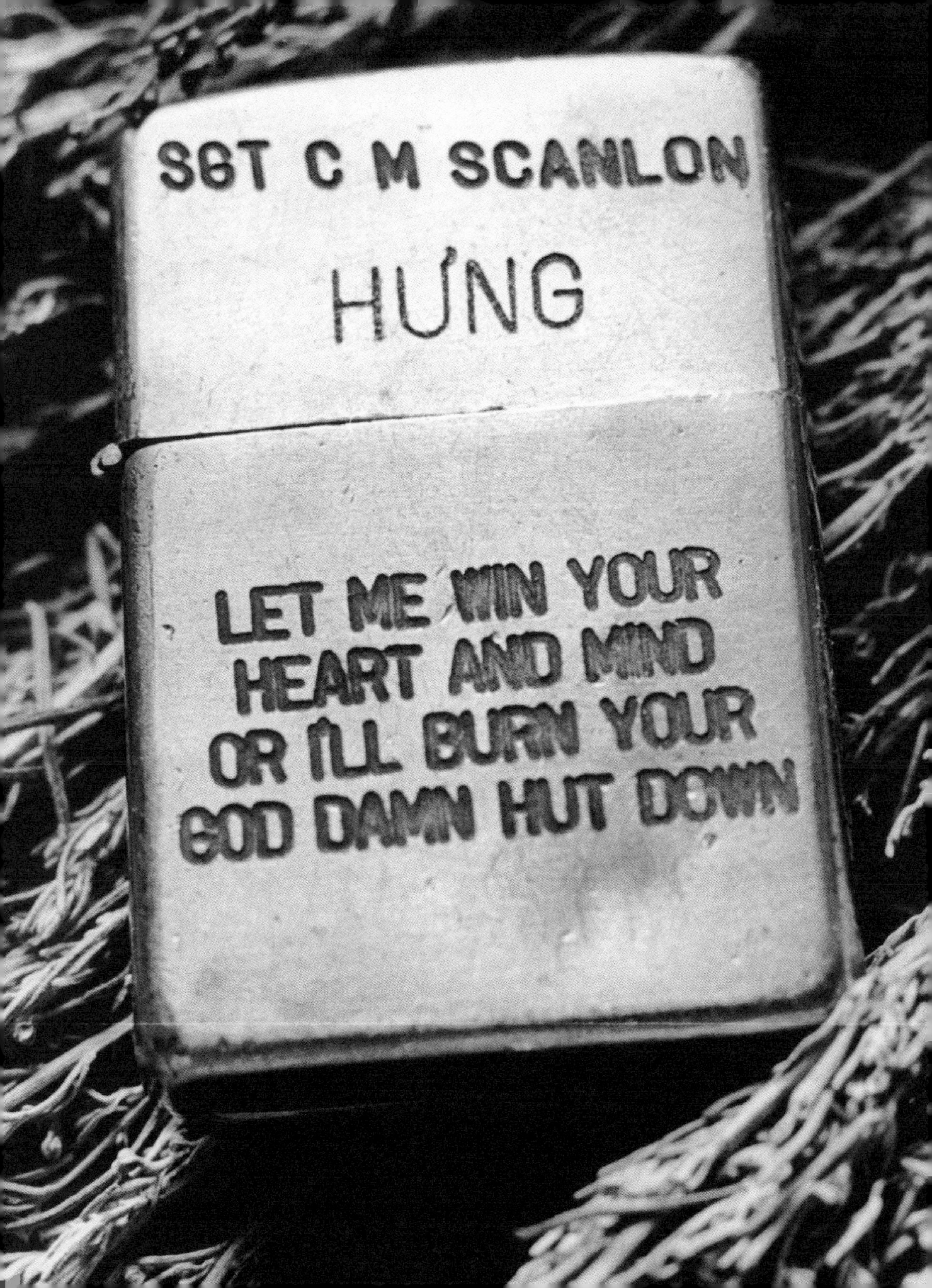
SGT C M SCANLON
HƯNG
LET ME WIN YOUR
HEART AND MIND
OR I'LL BURN YOUR
GOD DAMN HUT DOWN

LET THE ENEMY
TOUCH YOUR SKIM
AND YOU CUT IN TO
HIS FLESH LET HIM
CUT IN TO YOUR

FLESH AND YOU
PIERCE IN TO HIS
BONES LET HIM
PIERCE

IN TO YOUR BONES
AND YOU TAKE HIS
LIFE

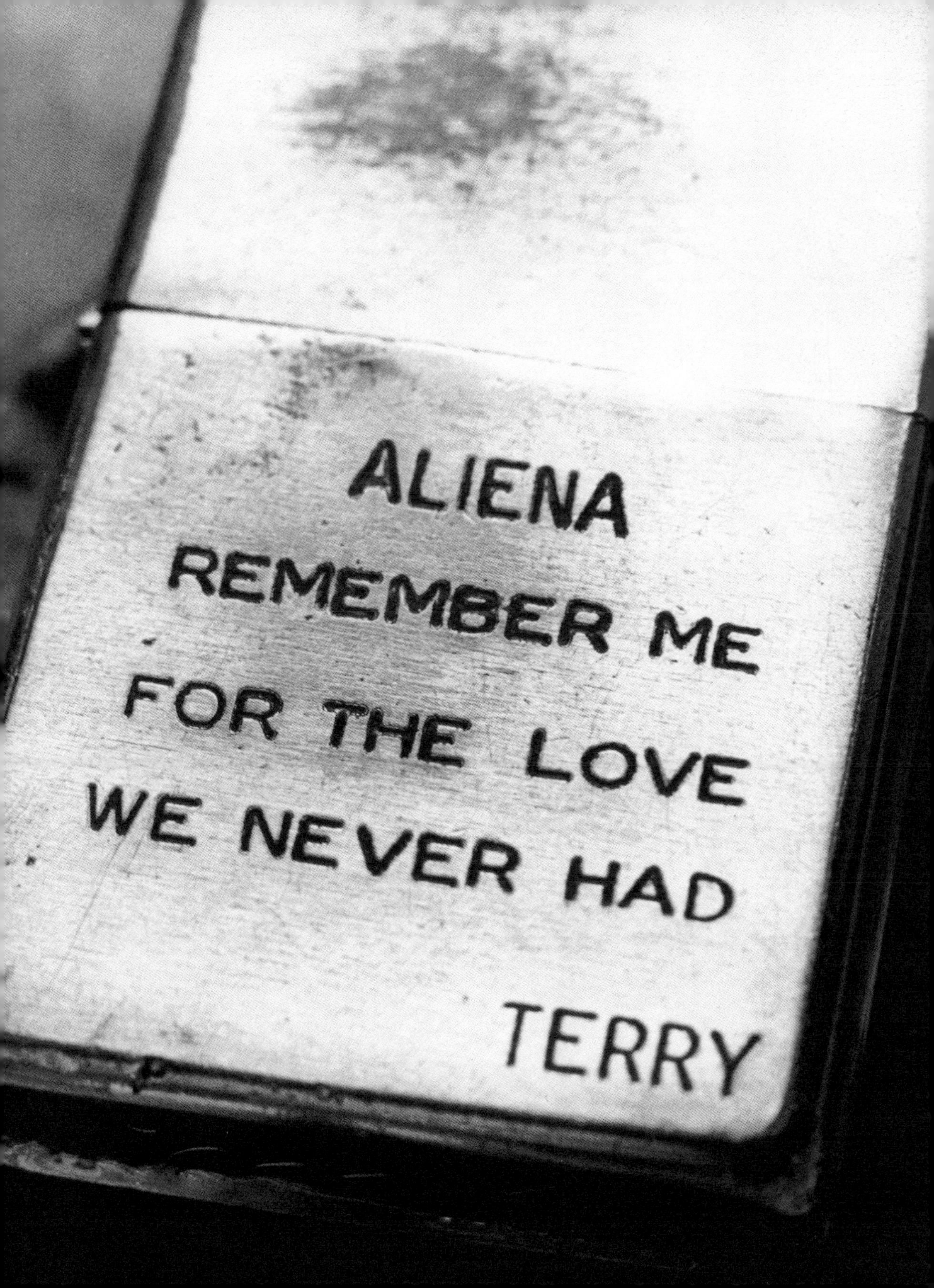
ALIENA
REMEMBER ME
FOR THE LOVE
WE NEVER HAD
TERRY

"Stay high and Keep low"

The Evening of Adam

I am Eve, great Adam's wife,
'Tis I that outraged Jesus of old;
'Tis I that robbed my children of Heaven,
By rights 'tis I that should have gone upon the Cross . . .

There would be no ice in any place,
There would be no glistening windy winter,
There would be no hell, there would be no sorrow,
There would be no fear if it were not for me.

From Come Hither, *ed. W. de la Mare*
(translated by Kuno Meyer)

W hat I don't understand," said Eve, "is how, while one person is—well, say, looking at the violets in a hedge, somewhere else another person will undoubtedly be torturing a third person to death. Do you see what I mean?"

"Well, not altogether," said Adam. "I don't quite see what you mean. No." He stubbed out a cigarette in his saucer and frowned with assumed concentration.

"At its simplest," she said, "what I think is that there is one god of the wild violets and the kittens, and possibly of the sunrise, and another of the torture chambers, and what worries me is that if I have to follow one I have to follow the one who allows the torture to take place. Do you see?"

"You mean you're a masochist," he suggested.

"No," she said, "that isn't what I mean."

"Then you mean you don't want to be seen as sentimental," he said with an air of one concluding an argument.

"Of course I don't," she said. "Don't be stupid."

"Do you mean you don't mean you don't want to seem sentimental?" he asked. "Or do you mean you don't want to be seen as sentimental? I only ask, because you tend to be a little unclear." He resented being called stupid.

"I'm not sentimental," she said.

"All girls are sentimental," he said, still resentful.

She said nothing. She had not yet learned that there was little to be gained from discussion with a person who does not share your views, or wish to, but she could think of nothing more to say: it was as difficult for her to express what she felt as to describe a dream.

"Do you want the last piece of cake?" he asked, his hand poised.

"Yes," she said.

"Well, you can't have it," he told her, and picked it up and bit it.

"I didn't really want it at all," she said, watching as he ate hastily, making sure of it.

"You don't want to get fat," he said, smiling, back at her.

"Nor do you," she said, "and you've got maraschino cherry sticking to your front teeth."

"I'm not the type who gets fat," he said.

She looked round the cafe: apart from themselves it was occupied only by middle-aged ladies in pairs. "There aren't any students," she observed, "except for you."

"We don't use this place much," he said, and she wondered why he'd brought her there.

"Are you ashamed of me," she asked, "or of the students?"

"You'd find the student dives affected," he said.

She pondered this, speculating on his opinion of her, the way he perceived her: she knew that he considered her uneducated, but sometimes she thought that perhaps he overrated her intelligence, for he often told her things she couldn't understand—philosophical things that he wanted to say to an appreciative listener; they did not require a response, only unquestioning acceptance and tacit agreement. Her own queries he disregarded, just as he dismissed her insights. He treated her as others treated clever pets, with affection and proprietorial pride, but never taking them as seriously as they would a member of their own species. His expectations of her intelligence were related only to his own needs. He had never had a real pet: nothing furred, scaled, or feathered had been permitted in his parents' house.

"Why would I find them affected?" she asked, although she knew already that he had decided that her innocence would be affronted by the self-conscious posturing of his peers.

"They're not your sort of thing," he said, "not your sort of thing at all."

"Do they have beards?" she asked, with what sounded like deliberate naïveté. Hearing herself, she added, "Because I was thinking about it on the train. I was thinking that beards were always considered a sign of virility and now only thin men who stoop have them—no elder statesmen, and no royalty except the one who married that big blonde. It's funny how fashions change." She wished she hadn't used the word "fashion," since it might give him the impression that she was interested in such things as hem lengths and hats. This would make matters difficult, necessitating further efforts to become visible, to be seen as she was in truth, rather than the way he wished her to be. She wanted him to love her for what she was. Honesty was a strong constituent in her character, although she sometimes thought this was only because she had an innate dislike of muddle and misunderstanding, and therefore it could not be construed as a virtue. Sometimes, too, she thought that perhaps it was vanity that compelled her to her Cromwellian stand: that anyone insisting that he must be portrayed with all his flaws might not be a simple, no-nonsense soldier-man, but one of such gross conceit that he must expose even his carbuncles to the watching world.

"I can't think of any with beards," he said, having considered her question. "They're out of style."

She opened her mouth to say she'd just said that, but decided against it. He hadn't been listening to her.

Two years later nothing had changed very much. They were married, he was teaching at one of the duller old-fashioned universities, had given up smoking, and got rather fat, and she was pregnant. She was no longer in love with him, but then after two years she had never expected to be. She was fond of him, and pregnancy, when she didn't think about it, made her feel like something to do with slow-moving streams through long-grassed meadows, cow-like but cleanly, so she was content up to a point, though with certain reservations.

There had been one disquieting development of which she was not yet aware. He had gradually grown to depend on her: on her daily presence—which was perhaps only to be expected—but also on her scrupulous candor. If she had known this it would have worried her, since she had never intended that her honesty should have any purpose but to reveal herself and do away with concealment. It was merely a tool, like a flyswatter, to keep confusion at bay. Now, however, he was reliant on it, although it would have taken him some time and effort to discover, realize, and admit that this was so—supposing he were ever prepared to undertake such an exercise.

"Eve," he said, one Sunday morning, and then was silent.

"Adam?" she prompted him after a while.

"What?" he said, looking up. "Oh nothing." He had been going to tell her about one of his more problematical students, perhaps even ask her advice, but then he had thought that, although she would undoubtedly give him her truthful views on the matter, still maybe she would be unable to perceive the subtleties involved. His opinion of her intelligence had grown increasingly warped as he grew more aware of her honesty.

She spent the morning with the washing machine, had a boiled egg and a tomato for lunch, and then went into the garden to sit under the greengage tree and wonder what the future held. The garden was separated from the surrounding fields by a dry, nettle-filled ditch—what, in a grander establishment, would have been called a ha-ha—and, for reasons she had never quite fathomed, it served its purpose. Cows, farm dogs, strangers never leapt into the ditch. She wondered if, when the baby started to crawl, he would fall in it and suffocate in stinging nettles, and whether the ditch itself would present as great a danger as the cows, dogs, and strangers would if it were not for the existence of such a barrier. Perhaps they should put up a fence or perhaps they should sell this house and move into the town, where more civilized hazards prevailed. The gamekeeper had already advised her to uproot the deadly nightshade and the lilies of the valley, anticipating the time when an inquisitive, greedy novice in the garden would range it from border to border, experimenting. Sometimes the thought of how much she would have to teach her child made Eve feel worried and tired. She was ignorant of the ways of babies.

The farmer was driving his tractor round and round the field behind her. Eve had no idea why he was doing this and no real desire to find out, so when he came level with her and stopped for a chat they discussed the political situation rather than the state of the crops, though the farmer did confide that he had had a bad experience only the other day, thus confirming Eve's suspicions that the rural way of life involved many arcane and unforeseeable dangers.

"Jones totaled the fertilizer," she told Adam that evening, as they sat under the greengage tree, drinking coffee. "The tractor hit something, so he baled out, but the fertilizer was a write-off. Isn't that interesting," she added, as he did not respond.

"What did he hit?" asked Adam, making an effort.

"Do you know, I didn't ask him," said Eve. "I can't think why."

Adam looked at her warily. She gazed at the bottom of the garden with an aloof, abstracted air until a mosquito whanged past her face and she struck out at it.

"I'm tired of the country," she said. "And it's no place to bring up a child. We should move back to town."

Adam was startled and—when he had considered for a moment—appalled. "What do you mean?" he asked. It was surely universally accepted that the countryside provided the best environment for child-rearing.

"It's unhealthy," said Eve, "and dangerous."

"The baby won't be driving a tractor," protested Adam.

Eve did not deign to reply.

"What do you mean by unhealthy?" he went on. "What's dangerous about it?" If he didn't know better he would have thought her capricious, but she had grown more serious of late: sometimes she seemed even morose. Her odd insights, when she expressed them (which she did with less frequency than previously) no longer pleased him with their strangeness, but rather alarmed him.

Eve, if he had asked her, might have explained that this was only to be expected: that a very young and pretty girl uttering truths makes them enchanting, whereas that same girl after some years of marriage will, in all probability, have learned different and deeper truths, and if she has any sense will keep them to herself. Young and pretty girls—Eve might have told him—can carry on any way they like, and should they be open and candid, as well as young and pretty—why, then they are irresistible. But as time goes by, the teller of truths gradually becomes threatening. It was unfortunate that Adam had loved Eve for her honesty, since he would, in time, find it unbearable.

Once he had kept her to himself for fear that someone would steal her from him; now he hesitated to expose his colleagues to her for fear of what she might say. He had made the mistake of imagining that her candor was not incompatible with tact, and was now discovering that nor was it compatible with charity—a far more serious matter when it came to social intercourse. He told people that his wife was given to unstudied utterance, to saying the first thing that came into her head, and he would laugh indulgently.

"The most dangerous thing about it," said Eve, "is that it's not the way you think it is. It's ruining my peace of mind." Here Adam remembered a time when Eve had announced that she was going to give the Master's wife a piece of her mind. He had asked if she was sure she could spare it, and Eve had laughed. He was not at all convinced that she would laugh now.

"What do you mean?" he asked again.

"I've got a picture of it," said Eve, "in my head. But when I open my eyes and look at it it isn't like that. In my head I see meadows of wild flowers, and clear water, and chickens, and dabbling in the dew makes the milkmaids fair, and dear old Dobbin and Farmer Giles—and public hangings and gibbeted corpses a bit—and ducking stools . . ."

"Sounds idyllic," interrupted Adam, perversely relieved to think that his wife might, after all, merely be slightly mad. He had no sense, and therefore no fear, of the terrifying honesty of lunacy, believing that truth, sanity, and reality represented aspects of the same whole.

"I've been reading about the past," said Eve. "I spent all my childhood reading about the past and it has had its effect."

"What did you ever read," asked Adam, "apart from *Winnie the Pooh*?"

"I don't like *Winnie the Pooh*," said Eve.

"You did once," said Adam, unwisely.

"No, I didn't," said Eve. "You're mistaking me for someone else. I liked *Mother Goose*." She got up and began to clear away the coffee cups.

"I'll do that later," offered Adam.

Eve didn't pause but, waddling slightly, made for the kitchen door. "Later isn't any good," she said, "when it's got to be done now."

"Why does it have to be done now?" asked Adam. Eve said nothing. If she had she might have said several things: that the smell of stale coffee sickened her, that the table looked untidy, that moths would founder in the dregs, or simply that later was always too late, especially in domestic matters. That, however, would have sounded puritanical while she wished only to be cutting.

"I liked Beatrix Potter too," she told Adam, when she went back to the garden, "I liked those pictures of cabbages and carrots in Beatrix Potter and I didn't mind all those dressed-up rabbits, but now I come to think of it I never could stand *Winnie the Pooh.*" She was not sure why it seemed so important to make this clear to her husband, and he was obviously not interested. "And I hated *Alice in Wonderland,*" she said. Adam stood up, yawning. Eve nearly divulged that she had enjoyed the *Arabian Nights,* but thought better of it.

"Time you were in bed," said Adam, but Eve knew that what he meant was that he was tired.

She lay awake while Adam slept and the baby explored its environment.

Eve was surprised when the baby was born. She had assumed it would be a boy and it was not. She was also surprised to learn how much pain the body could generate, the involuntary power of muscle, and most surprised of all to realize what love was. It was the quality and intensity of it which disconcerted her. Being Eve, of course, she had to try to explain her feelings.

During the third month of the child's life Adam seriously lost his temper. He had always been self-centered and irascible, but before the baby was born he had considered himself, albeit mistakenly, the center also of Eve's life. To do him justice, he had tried for a time to regard his changed situation reasonably, telling himself that all new mothers must inevitably become bound up in their offspring. He had tried to make allowances for Eve's distractedness, tiredness, and melancholy, until one evening when the baby was asleep he looked up to see that Eve, who was sitting on the sofa, had tears in her eyes. This annoyed him and he demanded to know what she thought she had to cry about. Instead of letting the tears fall and appealing for his sympathy, Eve told him. She did not explain that she was suffering from the depression which frequently results from the hormonal disarray consequent upon childbirth, nor that she was exhausted by sleepless nights, nor that she felt they were growing apart. To Eve all that was immaterial. She had, she said, opened her eyes and seen that there was nothing.

"What do you mean nothing?" demanded Adam in a towering rage, for this was something worse than ingratitude. "If you'd stop sniveling and blow your nose, maybe you'd see more clearly."

"I do see clearly," said Eve. "That's the trouble." Adam concluded that his wife was either mad or correct in her judgment. It was easier to believe the former.

"You're mad," he said.

Eve did not bother to argue but rose and went to bed.

The next day was Sunday and Adam had asked some people to come for a drink before lunch. The weather stayed fine and he carried bottles and glasses into the garden. The people were not very important—a visiting American professor and his wife, two of his better-bred students, and a retired don whose mind was going. Nevertheless, Adam had a word with Eve. "Eve," he said, "I know you've been under a strain . . ."

"No, I haven't," said Eve.

Adam snapped his mouth and his eyes simultaneously shut for a second, a trick he had when exasperated by a person who either contradicted or failed to comprehend him. "Whatever the reason, you've been depressed," he said, "and I don't want you coming out with a lot of nonsense and boring the Heimlichs with your miseries."

"I won't say a word," said Eve, who was not so far removed from ordinary human feeling that she couldn't take offense. She knew that Adam often found her an embarrassment, and she also knew that if it weren't for his attitude of mingled apprehension and apology many people would accept her at her own valuation. Adam behaved like an inexperienced ringmaster, introducing an exotic and unreliable exhibit to an inattentive audience. If he would leave her alone, all would be well.

"Do you mean I shouldn't knee them in the groin when they try to shake hands?" suggested Eve.

"You know what I mean," said Adam. "I mean just don't say things like that. Just try and be like everyone else." His tone was slow and slightly ominous. If he had examined his reactions to Eve at this moment he would have found that what he resented most particularly was her lack of respect for him. It had not yet occurred to him that she didn't love him, despite her obvious preference for the baby.

"And try and remember most people aren't very interested in babies," he said.

"A lot of women are," said Eve. "They have to be, really."

"A lot of women aren't coming," said Adam, cutting the argument short.

"I know they're not," said Eve under her breath. "Most of the women in the world aren't coming. Only one."

Adam, too, found his last remark ill-expressed and this annoyed him further. He was suffering the anxiety of the host who is about to expose his domestic arrangements to possibly critical view, and Eve was doing nothing to help. "What are you giving them?" he demanded.

Eve had once had a nanny who, when posed this question, would respond tersely, "Shit 'n' sugar." Eve, however, spoke the truth. "Olives," she said, "and bits of toast with lumpfish roe on, because we can't afford caviar."

"Nobody can afford caviar these days," said Adam, angered afresh at what seemed to be the implied complaint.

"That was caviar the other night," said Eve, "at the Johnsons'. That was beluga."

"I hate caviar," said Adam.

"I've prepared some sardines for you," said Eve, "with lemon and black pepper." But her tone was less conciliatory than matter of fact and did nothing to improve his mood.

The students were the first to arrive and Eve welcomed them sensibly. "You found us all right," she said. "The roads are quite clear on a Sunday."

Adam relaxed sufficiently to pour three glasses of wine without making a fuss about finding the corkscrew, which had been half concealed behind the bottles. "Except when they're harvesting," Eve continued, and Adam stiffened again. "When they're harvesting," said Eve, dreamily, "you can get stuck behind the hay truck for miles. It's rather peaceful. There's nothing you can do but follow it."

Adam interrupted. "You didn't pass Ludo, did you?" he asked. Ludo was the old don who was slowly but surely losing his mind.

"No, I don't think so, did we?" said the students generally, and to each other. "We didn't notice him. I didn't. Did you? No. I think we'd have noticed if we'd passed him."

"He will insist on driving himself," said Adam. "It's very worrying, but what can you do?" He stopped abruptly and glanced at Eve, who was quite capable of saying that you shouldn't ask him to come for drinks if you were worried about his driving. She smiled when she saw her husband looking at her and he realized she hadn't been listening. "Anything to eat?" he asked.

Eve looked briefly puzzled. "I told you," she said, "a minute ago. There's . . ."

"Well, shall we have it?" said Adam hastily. "Shall I help you bring it out?"

"Oh, I see," said Eve. "I wasn't going to bring it out yet in case the wasps get in it, but I'll bring the olives." She went into the cottage and was gone for so long that Adam went to find her.

"What are you doing?" he inquired.

"We've got a plague of ants," said Eve. "I've just noticed them. I think they're based under the sink and they come out on expeditions."

"Well, never mind them now," said Adam, impatiently. "We've got guests."

"You may have guests," said Eve. "I've got ants."

"Don't-be-so-bloody-stupid," said Adam, whispering. "Come-on-out-and-behave-like-a-normal-human-being."

"You don't understand," said Eve. "I think they may have got into the light refreshments. I just saw a bit of lumpfish roe move."

"I don't care," said Adam. "Just bring it out and don't mention it. Just come on." As he passed around the plates it occurred to him that he had been hasty. He should have told Eve not to say one word about ants, not to suggest that the guests might mistake fish eggs for ants' eggs, not to voice concern for the likely bewilderment of the small creatures. She might say anything. Already she was looking closely at the plate on the table. "Here are the Heimlichs," he said, too loudly, as they emerged from the shadowed path into the garden. "You found us all right." Then he wished he had let Eve say that. She had sounded quite ordinary and reasonable saying it to the students.

The Heimlichs had, by this time, seen many English country gardens and grown a little blasé about them. "I like your lupins," said Mrs. Heimlich.

"And this is a greengage, isn't it?" said the professor, tapping the tree with the stem of his pipe.

"Oh, you've got a baby," observed Mrs. Heimlich, catching sight of the basket on the garden bench. "Isn't he *cute.*"

"It's a girl, actually," said Adam, before his wife could speak.

"Hard to tell when they're so little, isn't it?" said Mrs. Heimlich, by way of excuse.

"Not if you know where to look," said Adam, and stopped, appalled, as he heard himself. It was one of Eve's remarks. She had said it at the christening, thus lowering the tone of the occasion quite unnecessarily.

"That's perfectly true," agreed Mrs. Heimlich, not at all disconcerted. Adam smiled uneasily. A normal woman, he thought, would have responded with distaste, would, at least, have withheld approval.

"Caviar?" he offered.

"I don't care for caviar, thank you," said Mrs. Heimlich, helping herself to an olive. Adam decided he didn't like her. It was quite probable that she would get on well with Eve.

"Deviled sardine?" he suggested sarcastically.

Mrs. Heimlich regarded him with an air of mild surprise. "I'm allergic to seafood," she said, as though he could have been expected to know that.

Eve listened tranquilly. She had met several educated American ladies and felt quite at home with their assumption that all human beings were equal, were much the same, and therefore should be able to communicate without undue explanation or heart-searching. Adam, she knew, found this unwomanly and unseemly. He thought that women should be modest and—if not exactly mysterious— should keep their mouths shut most of the time, partly because he thought they had nothing to say, but largely because what they did say confounded his expectations. Besides, Adam liked to do the talking.

"Hullo, Ludo," he said, as the mad don appeared, tottering slightly. "Eve, here's Ludo."

Eve was speculating on Mrs. Heimlich's possible reaction were she to become aware of Adam's attitude to the female sex. It would— mused Eve—be entertaining for a moment, but not conducive to a civilized atmosphere: it would disrupt the tenor of an academic English afternoon in the garden. Certainly these were sometimes fraught with ill-feeling, but it was usually occasioned by scholarly disagreements or personality clashes between the males present. At Adam's university, matters were still conducted in a traditional fashion and the ladies passed cucumber sandwiches, if a little desperately (many were on tranquilizers or drank in secret) and discussed among themselves such things as social work and the overwhelming need for the provision of more nurseries.

"*Eve,*" said Adam.

"Hullo, Ludo," said Eve. "Have a sardine."

Ludo chose a piece of toast with lumpfish roe on it. A fish egg broke away from the rest and settled on his chin.

"Ludo," said the students, "you are a messy old thing. Where's your handkerchief? Here, let me . . ." They bore him away to a shady corner and a garden seat where they sat him down and fussed about him in a motherly way.

"It's rather touching," said Mrs. Heimlich, "the way they're so good to each other. Homosexuals."

Her husband bent an indulgent if faintly nervous glance on her. "You're not supposed to say that, Nancy," he observed.

"Don't be ridiculous," said Mrs. Heimlich, consuming another olive.

"Wine?" asked Adam evenly.

"When I'm very old," said Eve, "I'd like to be looked after by a young man or two."

"Why is that?" asked the professor.

"I don't think they'd beat me up," said Eve. "Not if they knew and loved me well. There are grannies in the village who are black and blue because their families thump them for being tiresome."

"You don't know anything about it," said Adam.

"Jones told me," said Eve. "There's an epidemic of granny-bashing going on. You can hear their old bones crack in the evening when everyone comes home from work and wants to drink their tea in peace in front of the television and granny won't get out of the armchair. They seize her by her withered old leg and throw her down on the linoleum."

Mrs. Heimlich looked serious, but not unduly so.

"You should be more careful what you say," said Adam, but he was annoyed less by the possibly slanderous aspects of his wife's conversation than by what seemed to him to be its fantastic elements. Why, for instance, did she imagine the village houses to be furnished with linoleum?

"Ludo seems to think there's trouble brewing in Algeria," remarked the undergraduates, reintroducing themselves into the group and supporting the aged don between them.

"I'm sure he's right," said Professor Heimlich. "Islam is on the march."

"Ludo says fundamentalism in all its forms is undermining the proper bases of authority worldwide, don't you, Ludo? Yes, exactly. That's what Ludo says," said the undergraduates, setting him carefully down on another chair near the table.

"I'm afraid it's incontrovertible," agreed the professor, briefly arranging his face in an anxious frown to indicate that he appreciated the gravity of the situation. "You remember the quote from Yeats . . ."

"'The best lack all conviction while the worst are full of passionate intensity,'" chorused the undergraduates.

"We must never allow ourselves to fall into the trap of believing ourselves to be powerless," stated Mrs. Heimlich, with pious firmness.

"How d'you mean, honey?" inquired the professor. Adam's mouth hung open a little: it struck him as strange to hear a man encouraging his wife to air her views. He did not think Mrs. Heimlich particularly stupid (no more than most women) but he could not see that the ideas of *any* woman could be relevant in a discussion not concerned solely with frivolities.

"I mean that if we believe ourselves to be powerless," said Mrs. Heimlich, "we will have fallen into a trap. The enemy always takes advantage of an adversary's weakness." The Heimlichs shared a moment of respectful silence as they contemplated this insight.

"I know," said Eve, and would have continued, but Adam interrupted. "What did you think of Hudson's piece in the *TLS*?" he asked the professor, loudly. They fell into esoteric discussion, of interest only to those well-versed in their discipline, and left Eve and Mrs. Heimlich to amuse themselves with feminine topics.

"How do you put up with him?" asked Mrs. Heimlich, never one to beat about the bush.

"I'm not sure," said Eve. "I often wonder."

"You don't have to, you know," said Mrs. Heimlich.

"I do in a way," said Eve, "because the baby's small and I'm not qualified to do anything but put up with being married."

"Stuff and nonsense," said Mrs. Heimlich in an American manner.

"Besides," said Eve, "he's not all that bad." Mrs. Heimlich looked dubious. "Honestly," said Eve, "there are a lot of Englishmen who are worse." Mrs. Heimlich looked frankly incredulous.

"I know what you're going to say," Eve went on. "You're going to say it's all the fault of the public schools. You're absolutely right, of course."

"I was going to say," Mrs. Heimlich announced, vigorously, "that it's all the fault of English women. If the men are allowed to be arrogant and patronizing, then the women have a lot to answer for, letting them get away with it."

"I don't mind the arrogance and patronizing so much as how they can't put a washer on a tap," said Eve. "I have to do things like that myself, because Adam thinks it's beneath him, and anyway, he wouldn't know how to."

"Whatever happened to the New Man?" asked Mrs. Heimlich, but her tone was abstracted and her question rhetorical, requiring no answer apart from a sigh of agreement. Eve supplied this. Mrs. Heimlich bent closer and squinted at her through narrowed eyes. "You're too smart to go on with it for long," she said. "I've known a lot of women and I can tell the losers. You're no loser."

"It's interesting you should say that," said Eve, "because I'd have thought I was. I often feel very beaten and pointless. You do feel like that if nobody listens to you."

"But you're a smart girl," Mrs. Heimlich informed her. "You've got a brain."

Adam heard this word and thought it tactless. He glanced nervously at where Ludo sat flanked by his acolytes.

"Ludo says we must all watch Eastern Europe very carefully," said the young men. "Don't you, Ludo? He says the collapse of communism is going to leave a dangerous power vacuum. He sees no cause for rejoicing on the part of the West, do you, Ludo?"

Mrs. Heimlich and Eve listened in silence until Adam and the professor resumed their conversation. "Well, I could have told him that," said Eve, when it was safe to speak.

"You've got a brain," repeated Mrs. Heimlich, and Adam twitched.

Eve mused. She supposed it must be true since she had been half-consciously evaluating the guests in the garden and found them wanting. Even Mrs. Heimlich, of whom she was growing rather fond, could not be described as a great or original thinker, nor, if she was to be perfectly honest, was Mrs. Heimlich terribly interesting. This reflection made Eve feel guilty. "Have an olive," she said.

"Would anyone like the last of the caviar?" invited Adam, as he ate it.

The baby began to howl.

"There was an ant in that bit," said Eve.

Mrs. Heimlich smiled approvingly.

"Do something about the baby, can't you?" said Adam.

"Why don't you?" asked Mrs. Heimlich. "Why don't you do something?"

Adam ignored her.

Eve grew a little irritated with Mrs. Heimlich. It wasn't polite of her to point out Adam's deficiencies with such meticulous precision. It made Eve look a fool. She picked up the baby and carried her under the shade of the greengage tree.

Mrs. Heimlich followed.

"He's no good with the baby," said Eve. "She doesn't like him."

"That's terrible," said Mrs. Heimlich, but she spoke placidly, as one who was not greatly surprised.

"I don't think any men are any good with babies," said Eve, defiantly, putting Mrs. Heimlich in a dilemma.

While in her heart of hearts Mrs. Heimlich knew this to be broadly true, it was not, at present, received opinion in the circles in which she moved. In these circles it was held that men, if properly counseled, encouraged, and supported, would emerge as gentle, as able to express their emotions freely, able to weep without shyness and to engage in warm physical contact with other human beings without necessarily experiencing sexual arousal. She knew all this to be hogwash, but had never quite liked to say so since she adhered not to the orthodox but to the more liberal wing of feminism which allowed that men were human—if imperfectly so—and should not be the targets of too much destructive criticism, as this would be counter-productive. Looking however at Adam, Ludo, and the undergraduates, her instinct triumphed. "Nor do I," she said.

"Your one seems okay," said Eve, generous in response. Mrs. Heimlich bowed her head slightly in acknowledgement of the tribute. Her one, since he moved in the same social circles as herself, when outside the academic context, knew better than to speak or behave in a traditionally masculine fashion and never threw his weight about or snapped his fingers; within academia, the concept of political correctness was slowly bringing him to the first stages of mental instability, imperceptible as yet to the outsider, but evident to the wife who knew him. A neurotic inability to say what he meant was one of the signs. The outsider might consider such hesitancy to be the mark of the thoughtful, measured mentor, but his wife knew it was the result of fearing he might open his mouth and utter such words as cripple, or black, or girl, and find himself out of a job.

"He likes it here," she said. "He can relax. The pressures aren't so great."

"Really?" said Eve. "I don't know much about America, but I thought you were all more relaxed out there."

"Hah," said Mrs. Heimlich darkly.

"Indeed?" said Eve inquiringly.

"You have to watch your step," said Mrs. Heimlich, "every inch of the way."

"How tiresome," said Eve.

"You're not kidding," said Mrs. Heimlich.

"What are you girls doing?" asked Adam, coming upon them suddenly.

"We were discussing the state of the world," said Eve. "If you're looking for the wine it's either in the fridge or under the sink."

"Not for me," said Mrs. Heimlich. "We've got to get going." She rose from the grass and addressed her spouse. "Harold," she said.

"I know, honey," he said, hastening toward her. "We've got to get going."

"Us, too," said the undergraduates. "We have to go, too. Come on, Ludo. We have to go now."

"Goodbye," said Eve, "it was so good of you to come. It's been so pleasant." She brushed her hair out of the eye it was hanging over and smiled mildly. It made Adam nervous, that gentle smile.

He said, "Do you know, I heard the cuckoo earlier this year, introducing himself by his own name, like Americans do at dinner parties." Eve's smile faded. She turned back to the departing guests, none of whom seemed to have heard Adam's remark.

"Don't drink any more," she said, out of the corner of her mouth.

"I've hardly drunk anything," said Adam, and Eve, smiling again and waving, wondered if perhaps her husband, too, was going off his head.

A dam went to work on Monday morning and life began afresh for Eve. She knelt for a while in the kitchen watching the ants. They seemed to have some definite purpose in mind, she reflected. Or maybe she only thought that because it was said that they did, that they all worked together as one, performing their different tasks. This, of course, was nothing to the housewife whose duty it was to destroy them before they colonized the pantry shelves. She sprinkled a teaspoon of sugar on the floor and thought they paused to look up at her as though pondering her motive. Then she fed the baby mashed banana and yogurt and put her out in the garden under the greengage tree. She mopped the kitchen floor without looking to see whether she had drowned or discommoded any ants, for she liked to keep a clear conscience and was determined not to become overscrupulous in small matters. It did cross her mind that her impression of nothingness was erroneous and that lives as significant as her own were being played out under the kitchen sink, but she preferred not to dwell on it. The empty bottles clanked dismally as she put them in the garbage bag and she separated them with newspapers and banana peel. When she had made the bed she stood by the window looking down at the baby under the greengage tree, wondering what Mrs. Heimlich was doing today.

S o what have you been doing?" inquired Adam when he returned home.
　　"Nothing," said Eve.
　"Any chance of supper?" asked Adam, as the silence lengthened.
　"It's in the oven," said Eve, "but I must bathe the baby first."
　"Couldn't you have done that earlier?" inquired Adam.
　"No," said Eve.
　"Why not?" demanded Adam as she said no more and made no move.
　Eve sighed. "It would have been too early," she said, getting up and reaching for the baby where it lay on the grass on a woolly blanket.
　"I don't know what's the matter with you these days," said Adam.
　"I'm no different from what I ever was," said Eve. Adam was disposed to argue but found that he couldn't remember quite wherein lay the difference. He had a sense of imbalance, a lack of tension between himself and his wife. It was as though she had drifted invisibly, impalpably closer to him, beside him, behind him, so that he

could no longer see her clearly and she had ceased to have reality. "That was a good party yesterday," he said. "I think they all enjoyed it." He reminded himself that Eve had made an effort, had mashed up sardines and talked to the guests. "Shall I bathe the baby?" he offered suddenly.

"Oh no," said Eve. "I'll do it." She looked like a ghost in the twilight.

As she dried and powdered the baby and put her diaper on she wondered how it would be if Adam was doing it. He had on previous occasions talked to the baby in her bath, splashing her quite gently and squeezing the soap through his hands so it fell into the water, but he had never gone further than that, never picked her out all vulnerable and slippery to lie in his lap. Eve tried to picture the scene should she suddenly die without warning, insignificant as an ant, and lie on the bathroom floor, lifeless and useless. What would Adam do?

"What would you do if I died?" she asked as she pushed the peas toward him. He swallowed a piece of lamb chop and bit his tongue in irritation, thinking that she was asking him if he would marry again and forget her.

"How do I know?" he said crossly. "I suppose I'd have to marry again," he added, thinking that he was being unkind.

"Yes," said Eve, "I suppose you would. Have some more peas."

"No, thank you," said Adam. "They're rather dry."

"It's because they're real ones," said Eve. "They're nothing like as nice as frozen ones."

"Then why didn't you buy frozen ones?" said Adam.

"I thought these would be nicer," said Eve. Adam put down his fork and stared at her. Somewhere in the back of his mind he remembered that she had once been more interesting than this. He had never thought her particularly witty, but surely once she had talked about things other than the rival merits of fresh or frozen peas.

"I bought them the other day," said Eve, "and I shelled them myself." She had done it out of a sense of duty.

"I saw Heimlich today," said Adam. "We had a drink." He racked his brain for something of interest to tell his wife, to bring her out of the shadows where he could barely discern her. "He said his wife liked you very much."

"He could hardly say she hated me," observed Eve listlessly.

"He needn't have said anything," said Adam. "He needn't have mentioned you at all." He tried to remember if Heimlich had indeed said anything about Eve. He was almost sure he had but they had been speaking about Hudson's article in the *TLS* and Adam had been concentrating on that. He wished he could have a similar conversation with Eve, for there were aspects he still wished to clarify in his own mind, but she wouldn't understand the issues involved. "I wonder why fresh peas are no good," he said. "You'd think they would be."

"I'd like to go to college," said Eve. "I'd like to study philosophy."

"Don't be silly," said Adam. "You've got the baby to think about."

"I do think about her," said Eve, "but I'd like to think about something else as well." She knew what Adam would say eventually if she persisted, so she got up to move the dishes. He said it anyway.

"You haven't got that sort of mind."

"How do you know?" asked Eve. But she knew his reasons for saying it: he himself had that sort of mind and he didn't consider there was room in a relationship for two people with the same sort of mind. "What sort of mind do you have in mind?" she asked.

"The sort of mind that can *think*," said Adam.

"All sorts of mind can think," said Eve.

"Not yours," said Adam, enraged by this arrogant perception. "You've never had a thought in your life."

"Well, if that's what you think," said Eve, "I don't think you can think. Not very clearly anyway." She wondered if she would now become a victim of that domestic violence that Jones so often spoke of, for Adam was rising to his feet and his face had grown larger and red. He controlled himself with an effort and pretended he was merely leaving the table.

"Don't be silly," he said.

"All right," said Eve, "but I won't live in the country anymore."

W hy do you think I said that?" Eve inquired of the baby. "It wasn't true. I don't want to study philosophy. If I studied anything I'd rather study archaeology or dry stone walling. I'd like to study dressmaking. I don't want to do cake decorating or flower arranging, but I'd like to do something with my hands. Nothing too pretty but something clever. I'd like to make a tailored dress with inset panels. I wonder what it would look like if I sewed it all by hand with little tiny stitches. I wonder if Mrs. Heimlich would be pleased with me if I made it from beautiful, stiff material so that it almost stood up on its own. But you wouldn't like it. It wouldn't be comfortable for a baby and if I made it too stiff I wouldn't be able to sit down in it."

She picked up the baby and reflected on the sorrows of life, its brevity, which sometimes frightened her, and its seemingly interminable nature, which made her tired. "We'll go and have a look at the ants," she said to the baby. "As there is so much nature around we might as well commune with it a bit. Look . . ." she said, crouching on the floor half under the sink. "Look at all the little ants. They're like you, cootchie coo. Not very like you of course, because you're prettier, but they don't think too much. I don't think you think much, do you, baby? I hope not. It would be terrible if you were thinking when I thought you were just looking." She got up and straightened her skirt: it was made of soft cotton and fell in anarchic folds so that sometimes it was lifted by the wind, and sometimes impeded her walking. There was an ant on her hem. "There's one who wasn't looking where he was going," she informed the baby. "It's probably like me and it wants to get away and do something different. Or perhaps it knows what I'm planning and is escaping before I do it. It is my duty to wipe out this ant colony because this is Adam's house. A house built for human beings. We want no other form of life invading our territory." She threw the ant to the floor. "It could be a mad ant," she said. "An ant with learning difficulties. It might have been released into the community and the other ants have shunned it. I don't care . . ." she said. "I am not an asylum for mad ants. I have no fellow-feeling for it." She held the baby closely. "Don't worry," she reassured it. "I'm not at all mad. I'm not talking to myself. I'm talking to you."

When Adam came home he found that Eve had laid the garden table for supper. There was a jug of wild flowers in the middle of it and a bee hovered winningly about the petals of a pale antirrhinum.

"I don't know how you can suggest we should leave the country," said Adam contentedly, sitting down on the bench and stretching his legs.

"But have you not seen the backside of the angel?" asked Eve. Adam let his glance drift slowly towards her. He said nothing and Eve went into the house, returning at once with an earthenware casserole which she placed on a wooden coaster. She lifted the lid and he smelled herbs.

"It smells delicious," he said carefully.

"It is," said Eve. "It's lamb with apricots that have melted into the juice. The meat and the fruit are as one." She spoke matter-of-factly and went back to the kitchen for a bowl of rice.

"Salad?" asked Adam.

"Green salad," said Eve, "with garlic and oil."

Adam pondered this description as he ate. He wife's words, while unusual, were not ill-chosen: her account of this meal quite accurate. "It is delicious," he said.

"You never used to like fruit with meat," said Eve.

"Your cooking's improved," said Adam.

"The baby's asleep," said Eve.

"I'll open a bottle of wine," said Adam.

When she had cleared the things away Eve sat with her hands clasped round her knees and her soft skirt looking toward the fading horizon. "There's syllabub for pudding if you want it," she said. "Milk warm from the cow with lemon juice." She was thinking of the juice of lemons and the bitterness of rejection mingled with the foolish generosity of cream—the senseless, self-sacrificial way it rose to the top of the milk, ready to be skimmed.

"What do you mean—warm from the cow?" asked Adam. "You haven't been getting it straight from the farm, have you?" His tone was anxious and accusing.

"You can't get it straight from the farm," said Eve. "They won't let you. They take it all away and mess it all about in case it gives you diseases. I was using a figure of speech. They used to milk the cow into a bowl and rush back and put juice in it. Once they used to do that."

"Well, let's have some then," he said. The syllabub was delicious. He finished off the bottle of wine. "How was your day?" he asked.

Eve now considered for a while before she spoke. "It was partly very dull," she said, "and partly interesting. The baby's getting more interesting, but I don't know what to do about the ants. I did a lot of cooking—but then you know that. You just ate it. I think I'm going to have to pour boiling water on the ants. I swept them up with the dustpan and brush but they came back. The way they behave is quite interesting if you watch them for long enough."

"Then why do you want to pour boiling water on them?" asked Adam.

"Because you want to get rid of them," said Eve.

"Don't blame me for your sadistic tendencies," said Adam, and Eve went early to bed.

Adam sat up quite late wondering what his wife had meant by her remark about the backside of the angel. Perhaps she'd been quoting some obscure poem from some anthology of inferior verse. He hoped that she had. In the kitchen he noticed that she had left the dishes and pans unwashed. He bent down and looked under the sink to see if there was any sign of ants and, seeing none, rolled up his sleeves, filled the basin with hot water, and slowly washed all the dishes. He moved his feet hardly at all and then very carefully for fear of treading on Eve's ants.

The morning dawned fine. Adam hummed as he got dressed. Eve, lying on her side with a corner of the sheet in her mouth, wondered what the sound was: she had never heard a man humming before. She had never heard one singing on a private occasion, not even in the bath as they were reported to do. When they were first married Eve had often hummed, especially first thing in the morning, but Adam had told her it was an irritating habit. It was, Eve realized as she went into the kitchen. It was intensely irritating.

"What time will you be home?" she asked, to make him talk so that he would have to cease humming.

"What time would you like me to be home?" asked Adam, thinking that she must be planning a supper dish of such refinement that it required delicate timing and prompt attention.

But Eve said she didn't care what time he was home; not in an unfriendly or even impolite manner, but as one who respects the freedom of another to go his own way and make his own decisions about when he wishes to eat his supper.

Adam found it strangely frightening. There are cold and lonely aspects of freedom.

"I washed the dishes," he said.

"Thank you," said Eve, who was waiting for him to go so that she could wash them again properly. They were covered in a thin film of garlic-flavored grease.

"I thought I'd ask some people for a drink on Sunday," said Adam.

"If you do I'll kill myself," said Eve.

"Don't be silly," said Adam.

"I will," said Eve. "I will."

"I'll help you," said Adam, and went on to say that he would assist in tidying up and would do the shopping if she would just give him a list of what she wanted.

"Hemlock," said Eve.

"I'll ask the Heimlichs," said Adam.

When he had gone she stood in silence, but it was too quiet. "There is intelligent life under that sink," she said aloud.

Adam and Professor Heimlich had lunch together in the pub. Adam said, "I'm worried about Eve."

Professor Heimlich said, "Don't worry. Would you like another pint?"

Adam had another pint and the other half of the professor's sandwich, for Professor Heimlich was watching his weight. As he spoke, Adam realized that it was out of character for him to talk about his wife: it indicated, he thought, a previously concealed sensitivity in his personality, a maturity that he had not before been required to make evident. Perhaps almost a feminine side; something gentle and compassionate that had lain dormant until called upon. "She seems a bit low," he said.

"Maybe she spends too much time on her own," said the professor, glancing round to see if any other of his colleagues were lunching in this rather unappealing pub.

"She's not gregarious," said Adam. "She likes being on her own. She potters round the garden."

If this was the case, the professor couldn't see what the problem was. "Women are tougher than you think," he observed.

Relieved, Adam agreed that this was probably so.

She washed the dishes and she washed the baby and she washed the clothes. She washed her T-shirt and her cotton skirt and left them lying on the draining-board. Nothing—she thought. Now there's nothing to do. She went into the garden and back into the house, and then into the garden again. She looked at the pansies and they beamed back at her. They don't mean it, she thought. They reminded her of the university women, some of whom were ardent feminists who tended to cluster like pansies, beaming. She wondered what the torturer was doing at this moment and what God thought about it all.

"I'm going to sing you a song, baby," she said and lifted up her voice. "I'm a little prairie flower, growing wilder every hour. Nobody can cultivate me. Whoops, I'm a pansy." She became aware of the tractor in the field. "Where there is a tractor in this vicinity," she said under her breath, "there will undoubtedly also be a Jones. We must take evasive action," and she went back into the house, clutching her baby tightly. She knelt down and put the baby on a rug. "If I get under the sink," she said, "then if Jones comes begging for tea and cake he won't see me. And if he does, if he has the nerve to walk in and find me, I'll just say I was sorting out the ants."

After a while came the voice. "You there?" he called. "Anybody home?" Eve stayed quite still, her finger to her lips. Even when he'd gone she still crouched on the cold floor feeling closer to the ants.

"The noonday devil," she said, "is worse than the business that stalketh about in the dark, even more frightening than whoever it is who comes to walk in the garden in the cool of the evening."

How glad I am, she thought, that I didn't say that to Adam, for he wouldn't have understood. She reflected that she could have said it to Mrs. Heimlich, who would probably have thought her imaginative, whereas Adam would have considered her crazy. But better on the whole—she decided—just to say it to myself.

J ones, in his turn, went to lunch in the pub. "Crazy," he told his friends. "Mad. One minute she's singing her head off in the garden and the next she's sat under the sink with her head in her hands. I saw her through the window and I yelled through the door and she took not a bit of notice." He was aggrieved, having thought her friendly.

"Probably her time of the month," said his friends.

"Yeah," agreed Jones.

B ecause," said Eve earnestly to Mrs. Heimlich. "Sometimes the garden seems less like a garden than a charnel house." She was trying to make herself clear. "The flowers don't live very long and then they die and I see it all the time. I see winter coming, and then when it's spring those silly flowers think it's time to come out again."

"It's the progression of the seasons," said Mrs. Heimlich. "It's inspired poets through the ages. You should write."

"It's the earth," said Eve. "Things come out of the earth and then they go back into it and what, you wonder, what on earth is the point?" She looked fearfully to where the baby lay, separated from the terrible earth by a woolly blanket.

"You may still be suffering," said Mrs. Heimlich, "from post-partum melancholy. Nobody ever takes it sufficiently seriously."

"If I am," said Eve, "I think I've always had it. Ever since I was born myself. Perhaps everyone everywhere suffers from it always."

T he drinks party was similar to the last one, the same people present with the exception of Ludo, who, it seemed, was particularly confused at the moment. There was another difference: Adam had tied a tea towel about his waist and had made ham sandwiches. Occasionally he hummed.

"He's taken over the catering," said Eve. "God knows what's got into him. He says he wants to help but he's a nuisance. His ham sandwiches are horrible."

"And we're Jewish," said Mrs. Heimlich, adding, "womb envy."

"Pardon?" said Eve.

"He's trying to prove he can do whatever you can do," explained Mrs. Heimlich. "He envies your womb."

"He's welcome to it," said Eve.

"No, he's not," said Mrs. Heimlich. "It makes you appear redundant."

"I thought that was what women were supposed to do to men," said Eve.

"It works both ways," said Mrs. Heimlich, "in the battle of the sexes."

"Another sandwich?" Adam offered.

"Thank you, no," said Mrs. Heimlich.

"I want to live in a city," said Eve. She thought this sounded a little bald and rephrased it. "How I long to go back to the city." She looked toward the opening of the path that led away from the garden. "He won't let me," she said.

Mrs. Heimlich naturally assumed she was speaking of her husband, being unaware that Eve descried a dim yet implacable form poised not to exclude but to imprison her. "You tell him," she advised.

"I sometimes think he's the foul fiend," said Eve, and shivered, for images of the vile god Pan assailed her in the summer's heat.

"We all think that sometimes," said Mrs. Heimlich reassuringly.

The professor strolled over to them. "The boys seem to think Ludo's not long for this world," he remarked.

"Lucky him," said Eve.

"You mustn't talk like that," said the professor. "Here you are in this little earthly paradise. . . ."

The Heimlichs sat side by side in bed. "Adam said he was worried about her," observed the professor, "only the other day." Mrs. Heimlich said nothing.

"I never imagined things were as bad as that," he went on. "Poor Adam." Mrs. Heimlich lay down and gazed at the ceiling.

CONTRIBUTORS

Hilton Als is a contributing editor to *Grand Street*.

Amiri Baraka (LeRoi Jones) has written poetry, drama, novels, and essays. He is a political activist and a Professor of Africana Studies at the State University of New York at Stony Brook. His most recent works are *Wise/Why's/Y's*, a book of poetry from Third World Press, and *Transbluesency: Selected Poems* (Marsilio Press). *Black People & Jesse Jackson: Essays 1972–1988* and *Eulogies* (a collection of eulogies Baraka has given over the last twenty-five years for people such as Miles Davis, James Baldwin, Dizzy Gillespie, and William Kunstler) will be published in early 1996.

Martine Bellen's work has recently appeared in *The Gertrude Stein Awards for Innovative North American Poetry Anthology* (Sun & Moon Press), *Conjunctions*, and *New American Writing*. *Belle Starr* is excerpted from her forthcoming book of poetry, *Wild Women*.

Brigid Berlin lives in New York and is still organizing. A show of her work will be held at the Stubbs Gallery, New York in March 1996.

Bruce Berlind's translations of contemporary Hungarian poetry include *Selected Poetry of Ágnes Nemes Nagy* (University of Iowa Press), *Birds and Other Relations: Selected Poetry of Dezső Tandori* (Princeton University Press), Imre Oravecz's prose poems *When You Became She* (Xenos Books), and Ottó Orbán's *The Journey of Barbarus* (forthcoming from Three Continents Press). The Dana Professor of English Emeritus at Colgate University, he was awarded the Hungarian PEN Memorial Medal in 1986.

Jean Boivin is a Professor of Musicology at the Université de Sherbrooke in Quebec. He recently received the Grand Prix du Syndicat de la Critique Dramatique et Musicale. He is the author of *La Classe de Messiaen* (Christian Bourgois, 1995), from which the article in this issue of *Grand Street* has been excerpted and translated.

Pierre Boulez was born in Montbrison, France in 1925. After studying mathematics, he was admitted, in 1944, to the harmony class taught by composer Olivier Messiaen at the Paris Conservatory. Two years later, he became the musical director of the Renaud-Barrault Company and began to compose seriously. He was the chief conductor of the BBC Symphony Orchestra from 1971 to 1975, and in 1971, he succeeded Leonard Bernstein as the music director of the New York Philharmonic.

In 1972, French president Georges Pompidou appointed Boulez founder and director of the Institut de Recherche et de Coordination Acoustique/Musique (IRCAM). He went on, in 1976, to found the Ensemble InterContemporain, which he conducts regularly. His own compositions have been performed internationally and he received three Grammy Awards for a 1994 Bartók recording with the Chicago Symphony. A new production of Schoenberg's *Moses and Aaron*, conducted by Pierre Boulez in collaboration with Peter Stein, opened at the Amsterdam Opera in October 1995 and will be taken to the Salzburg Festival in August 1996. His essay *Periform* was published in French in Boulez's collection *Points de repère I: Imaginer* (Christian Bourgois, 1995).

Francesco Clemente is a painter and lives in New York and India.

Peter Cole is the author of *Rift*, a collection of poems. He is also the translator of *Selected Poems of Shmuel HaNagid* which will be published by Princeton University Press in January 1996.

Anne Doran lives in New York. She is currently writing and painting.

J. S. Drucker is a surf specialist for the State of California. He travels around and occasionally has a lucky find. He currently resides in Santa Monica, California.

Alice Thomas Ellis was born in Liverpool, England and was educated at the Liverpool School of Art. She is the author of *The Sin Eater* (1977) and *The Birds of the Air* (1980), both of which received a Welsh Arts Council Award, as well as *The 27th Kingdom*, which was nominated for the Booker Prize. Her book, *The Summerhouse Trilogy*, won the 1991 Writers Guild Award for Best Fiction, and her short story collection, *The Evening of Adam*, was published by Viking UK in 1994. She is the fiction editor of Duckworth Publishers and has seven children.

Clayton Eshleman's most recent collection of poetry is *Under World Arrest* (Black Sparrow Press). His translation of some of Artaud's late works, *Watchfiends & Rack Screams*, was recently published by Exact Change Press. Eshleman is a Professor in the English Department at Eastern Michigan University, where he edits *Sulfur* magazine. This June, with Gary Snyder, he will lead a tour to the Upper Paleolithic caves of southwestern France.

Celia Gilbert is the author of two books of poetry, *Bonfire* and *Queen of Darkness*. She is the winner of the Discovery Award, the Pushcart Prize IX, the Emily Dickinson Prize, and the Consuelo Ford Award from the Poetry Society of America. Her poems have appeared in *Poetry, The New Yorker, The Threepenny Review*, and *Southwest Review*, among others. The poems in this issue are part of a book-length sequence of poems. She lives in Cambridge, Massachusetts.

Arthur Goldhammer has translated more than sixty works from the French. He is currently translating *Les Platters* by Emmanuel Le Ore Ladurie.

Aysenur Güvenir was born in Istanbul in 1969, and studied translation and interpretation at Bogaziçi University. She is currently the coordinator of the written translation department of the Council of Interpretation and Translation in Istanbul. Her Turkish translation of Theodore Roethke's poetry will be published in 1996.

Shmuel HaNagid (993-1056 C.E.) was the first major poet of the Hebrew literary renaissance of Moslem Spain. HaNagid was also the Prime Minister of the Muslim state of Granada, battlefield commander of the non-Jewish Granadan army, and one of the leading religious figures in a medieval Jewish world that stretched from Andalusia to Baghdad. *Selected Poems of Shmuel HaNagid* will be published by Princeton University Press in January 1996.

Dennis Hopper is a film director, photographer, painter, and actor who appeared most recently in *Waterworld, Speed*, and *Red Rock West*. The movies he has directed include *Easy Rider, Colors, The Hot Spot*, and *Chasers*. Exhibitions of his visual work have been held in Barcelona, Paris, Boston, New York, and Los Angeles.

Adrienne Kennedy received a Lila Wallace Reader's Digest Award and a 1994 Award in Literature from the American Academy of Arts and Letters. Her plays are currently in a year-long run by the Signature Theater Company at the New York Public Theater. She lives in New York City.

Edward Kienholz was born in 1927 on a farm in Fairfield, Washington, near Spokane. He took to the road in the 1940s, working as a car salesman, an attendant in a state mental hospital, and a nightclub and restaurant proprietor. Kienholz's self-taught, artistic techniques reflect the practical skills he acquired in these varied occupations. By the early 1960s, he was assembling found objects in figurative environments and tableaux, which presented views of the underbelly of American society that ranged from the comically absurd to the tragically horrific. Walter Hopps, with whom Kienholz cofounded the Ferus Gallery in Los Angeles in late 1956, organized two major retrospective exhibitions of Kienholz's work, the first at the Pasadena Art Museum in 1961 and the second at the Corcoran Gallery of Art, Washington, D.C., in 1967. In 1973, Kienholz was awarded a D.A.A.D. (Deutscher Akademischer Austauschdienst) fellowship in Berlin and began to divide his time between Idaho and Berlin. In 1981, he publicly announced his collaboration with Nancy Reddin Kienholz, and all works from 1972 onward are signed with both of their names. An exhibition exploring his formative years, *Edward Kienholz: 1954–1962*, curated by Walter Hopps, opened at The Menil Collection, Houston in October 1995, and will expand to become *Kienholz: A Retrospective*, the first full-scale survey of the work of Edward and Nancy Reddin Kienholz, which will open at the Whitney Museum of American Art, New York in February 1996, and travel to The Museum of Contemporary Art, Los Angeles and the Berlinische Galerie, Berlin. Edward Kienholz died in Hope, Idaho in 1994. Nancy Reddin Kienholz continues to live and work in Hope.

Mária Kőrösy has an M.A. in English Literature from Budapest University. She has collaborated with Bruce Berlind on translations of Hungarian poets for nearly twenty years.

Onat Kutlar was born in Turkey in 1936. His first collection of short stories was published when he was eighteen. He also published one volume of poetry, *Perah Bir Aşk İçin Divan* (1981), two collections of essays, *Yeter ki Kararmasun* (1984) and *Bahar Isyancidir* (1986), and four screenplays. As a member of the executive board of the Istanbul Culture and Art Foundation, he founded the annual Istanbul theater festival. In 1968, he became editor-in-chief of the magazine *Yeni Sinema (New Cinema)*. On December 30, 1994, he was severely wounded, while drinking coffee at the Marmara Hotel in Istanbul, by a bomb planted by radical Muslims. He died eleven days later.

Okura Kyojin is a poet and sculptor living in Hiroshima. He studied in Madison, Wisconsin in the 1980s.

CONTRIBUTORS

James Laughlin's *The Country Road,* a book of poetry, was published by Zoland Books in October 1995.

Susie Mee has published a novel, *The Girl Who Loved Elvis,* the paperback edition of which will include *The Gospel According to Elvis,* and a book of poetry, *The Undertaker's Daughter.* She recently edited a book of stories by southern women writers called *Downhome* (Harcourt Brace).

Olivier Messiaen was born in Avignon, France in 1908. One of the most important composers of the twentieth century, he was also, from 1941 to 1977, a Professor of Composition at the Conservatoire de Paris. At the Conservatoire, he directed a class on analysis, harmony, and composition, and contributed to the education of some of the most important composers of the century: Pierre Boulez, Iannis Xenakis, Karlheinz Stockhausen, Gilbery Amy, and Gilles Tremblay, among others. He died in April 1992.

Hilda Morley is the author of several books of poetry, most recently *Between the Rocks,* published in a limited, fine-press edition by Tangram Press. She has received grants from the Guggenheim Foundation, the New York State Foundation for the Arts, and other organizations. Her book *To Hold My Hand* received the first Capricorn Award. She is currently working on a new volume of poems and a biographical memoir of her late husband, the composer Stefan Wolpe.

Gerard Mortier was born in Ghent, Belgium in 1943. After completing a doctorate in law at the University of Ghent, he worked at the Festival of Flanders and at the Opera of the Municipal Theatres of Frankfurt, before becoming artistic director of the Hamburg State Opera in 1977. From 1979 to 1981, he was artistic director of the Théâtre National de l'Opéra de Paris, and in 1981, he became artistic director of the Théâtre Royal de la Monnaie in Brussels. In 1985, he was appointed project director of the Bastille Opera in Paris by Jacques Lang. He is currently artistic director of the Salzburg Festival.

Tosa Motokiyu was born in Hiroshima, Japan in 1955. He studied musical composition in Milwaukee and Madison, Wisconsin in the early 1980s. Since 1984, he has lived alternately in Japan and Sebastapol, California, and has been engaged in translating and editing the manuscripts of Araki Yasusada.

CONTRIBUTORS

John Nathan is the Takashima Professor of Japanese Cultural Studies at the University of California at Santa Barbara and the translator of many of Kenzaburo Oe's works. His conversation with Kenzaburo Oe took place in April 1995 at the Japan Society in New York.

Ojiu Norinaga is a doctoral student in Comparative Literature. He currently lives in Tokyo, where he teaches English at the Nippon School of Business.

Kenzaburo Oe was born on the Japanese island of Shikoku in 1935. His novels include *The Silent Cry, A Personal Matter, Teach Us to Outgrow Our Madness,* and *Nip the Buds, Shoot the Kids.* His stories *The Way of Eating Fried Sausage* and *A Map of the World* appeared in issues 38 and 43 of *Grand Street.* He was awarded the 1994 Nobel Prize for Literature. His novella *J,* from which the story in this issue of *Grand Street* is excerpted, will be published by Blue Moon Books in 1996. His conversation with John Nathan, which also appears in this issue, was held in April 1995 at the Japan Society in New York.

Imre Oravecz was born in Szajla, Hungary in 1943. He graduated from Kossuth Lajos University of Debrecen with a Master of Arts degree in Hungarian and German Language and Literature, and pursued graduate studies in linguistics at the University of Illinois at Chicago Circle. He has been a Visiting Fellow at the University of Iowa and a Fulbright Lecturer at the University of California at Santa Barbara. Oravecz has published six books of poetry, most recently *Selected Poems.*

Suzan-Lori Parks's new play *Venus,* directed by Richard Foreman, will premiere at The Yale Repertory Theatre in March 1996, and will then open at The Public Theatre in New York in April 1996. Her first feature film, *Girl 6,* directed by Spike Lee, will also open in the spring of '96 at a theater near you.

Julian Reynolds was born in London in 1962. From 1985 to 1994, he was assistant musical director at the Netherlands Opera, where he conducted performances of Bartók's *Bluebeard's Castle,* Verdi's *Luisa Miller,* and Mozart's *Mitridate Re di Ponto.* In 1993, he conducted Brigitte Fassbaender's production of Britten's *A Midsummer Night's Dream.* He is a regular guest conductor for the Mariinsky Theater in St. Petersburg. As a pianist, he has recorded the complete works for piano and violin of Beethoven, Schubert, and Schumann for Globe Records with violinist Johannes Leertouwer.

Julian Schnabel is a painter and makes a good bowl of spaghetti.

Danny Tisdale was born in Compton, California in 1958, and moved with his family to Simi Valley in 1969 after the Watts riots. His eldest brother was a Green Beret in the Vietnam War and now serves in the Los Angeles Police Department; another brother and sister were Black Panther Party members. His work has been exhibited in *Malcolm X: Man, Ideal, Icon* at the Walker Art Center in Minneapolis in 1992, in *Black Male: Representations of Masculinity in Contemporary American Art* at the Whitney Museum of American Art in 1994, and in *Civil Rights Now* at the Southeastern Center for Contemporary Art in Winston-Salem, North Carolina in 1995. He is currently running for election to New York City Council in District #9, Harlem.

Javier Tomeo was born in Quicena, Spain in 1931. He studied Law and Criminology in Barcelona, where he now lives. He has published six volumes of fiction, including *Problemas Oculares* (Anagrama), in which the two stories published in this issue of *Grand Street* originally appeared. His work has been translated into several languages, and his novel *Amado monstruo* was adapted for the theater in France and Germany.

Luk Van Haute was born in Dendermonde, Belgium in 1963. He received a degree in Japanese Studies from the University of Ghent in Belgium. He lived in Japan for six years, two years of which he was a fellow at the University of Tokyo, researching contemporary Japanese literature, with a focus on Kenzaburo Oe. He currently lives in Ghent, where he works as a freelance writer and translator.

David Foster Wallace's novel *Infinite Jest*, from which *Chivalry* is excerpted, will be published by Little, Brown in February 1996.

John Waters lives in Baltimore, Maryland, where he is writing the script for his new movie. An exhibition of his photographs, *My Little Movies*, was held at American Fine Arts, Co., New York in 1995.

Jason Weiss is the author of *Writing at Risk: Interviews in Paris with Uncommon Writers* (University of Iowa Press, 1991). His translation of Marcel Cohen's *Mirrors* will be published by Sun & Moon Press in 1997. He is currently finishing his first novel.

Araki Yasusada was born in Kyoto, Japan in 1907 and moved to Hiroshima in 1921. In 1936, he was conscripted into the Japanese Imperial Army and worked as a clerk in the Hiroshima division of the Military Postal Service. His wife and youngest daughter died instantly in the atomic blast on August 6, 1945. His other daughter died three years later of radiation sickness. His son, who was nine months old at the time, was with relatives outside the city. Although Yasusada was active in avant-garde groups such as Ogiwara Seisensui's Layered Clouds and the experimental renga circle Oars, his work, along with that of his renga collaborators, Akutagawa Fusei and Ozaki Kusatao, is virtually unknown. Yasusada died in 1972 after a long struggle with cancer. In 1980, his son discovered fourteen spiral notebooks filled with poems, drafts, English class assignments, diary entries, recordings of zen dokusan encounters, letter drafts, and other fragments. The selections printed here are part of a much larger collection that is currently being prepared for book publication by his translators Tosa Motokiyu, Okura Kyojin, and Ojiu Norinaga. A volume of selected poems will be published in the United Kingdom by Spectacular Diseases.

Grand Street would like to thank
the following for their generous support:

Cathy and Stephen Graham
Barbara Howard
Dominic Man-Kit Lam
The National Endowment for the Arts
Suzanne and Sanford J. Schlesinger
Betty and Stanley K. Sheinbaum

ILLUSTRATIONS

front cover Julian Schnabel, *Veramente Bestia V (girl with no eyes)*, 1988. Oil on found painting, 20 x 16 in. Photograph by Phillips/Schwab. Courtesy of the artist and PaceWildenstein, New York.

back cover Dennis Hopper, *Untitled*, 1995. Color photograph, 11 x 14 in. Courtesy of the artist.

title page Dennis Hopper, *Untitled* (detail), 1995. Color photograph, 11 x 14 in. Courtesy of the artist.

p. 10 Photograph courtesy of Photofest.

pp. 14–15 *Josephine Baker in character*, 1936. Photographs courtesy of AP/Wide World Photos.

pp. 25–32 Julian Schnabel, *The Conversion of St. Paolo Malfi, near Rome, 1995*. Titles, dates, media, and dimensions appear on **p. 24**. Photographs by Julian Schnabel Studio. Courtesy of the artist and PaceWildenstein, New York.

pp. 82–88 Edward Kienholz, *Concept Tableaux*. **p. 82** Engraved bronze plaque, 9 x 13 ½ in. **p. 83** Framed description, 12 x 9 ¼ in. **p. 84** Engraved bronze plaque, 9 x 13 ½ in. **p. 85** Framed description, 12 x 9 ¼ in. Collection of Nancy Reddin Kienholz. **p. 86** Engraved bronze plaque, 9 x 13 ½ in. **p. 87** Framed description, 12 x 9 ¼ in. **p. 88** Interior view of *The State Hospital*, 1964–1967. Tableau: two plaster-cast/fiberglass figures, hospital beds, bedpan, hospital table, goldfish bowls, live goldfish, lighted neon tubing, steel hardware, wood, and paint, 96 x 144 x 120 in. Collection of Moderna Museet, Stockholm.

pp. 108–112 John Waters, *Self-Portrait*, 1994. Media and dimensions appear on **p. 112**. Courtesy of the artist and American Fine Arts, Co., New York.

pp. 121–128 Dennis Hopper, *Mardi Gras, Venice, Italy, 1995*. Eight untitled color photographs, **p. 121, p. 125, and p. 128** 14 x 11 in. **p. 122, p. 123, p. 124, p. 126, p. 127** 11 x 14 in. Courtesy of the artist.

pp. 134–139 Olivier Messiaen, pages from the score of *Catalogue d'oiseaux: X. Le Merle de roche (monticola saxatilis)*, 1956–58. Courtesy of Editions Musicales Alphonse Leduc, Paris.

p. 134 *Olivier Messiaen at work in the field notating birdsong by ear*, circa 1960. Black-and-white photograph, 12 ⅜ x 9 ½ in. Courtesy of Editions Musicales Alphonse Leduc, Paris.

p. 137 *Horned Owl*, from *The Book of Nature: Embracing A Condensed Survey of the Animal Kingdom as well as Sketches of Vegetable, Anatomy, Geology, Botany, Mineralogy, &c., &c., Volume 1*. Edited by an association of Scientific Gentlemen of Philadelphia. Published by Samuel C. Atkinson, Philadelphia, 1834.

p. 140 Color photograph, capture (enlargement) from videotape, 3 x 5 in. Photograph by Darryl Turner.

p. 156 Black-and-white photograph, 8 x 10 in. Copyright © Donna Van Der Zee. All rights reserved. Courtesy of Donna Van Der Zee.

pp. 161–168 Danny Tisdale, *The Black Museum*. Titles, dates, media, and dimensions appear on **p. 160**. **pp. 161–164, and p. 167** From *The Black Museum*, 1990. **p. 165, p. 166, and p. 168** From *The Last of the African-Americans*, 1994. Photographs by Tisdale Studio. Courtesy of the artist.

p. 195 *Belle Starr (Shirley)*, undated. Black-and-white photograph, 5 x 7 in. Courtesy of The Denver Public Library, Western History Department.

pp. 201–208 Brigid Berlin, *The Cock Book*. Titles, dates, media, and dimensions appear on **p. 200**. Photographs by Lary Lamé. Courtesy of Vincent Fremont Editions, New York.

pp. 215–220 J. S. Drucker, *Only the Heads Survive: Zippo Lighters from the Vietnam War*. Six black-and-white photographs, 8 x 10 in. each. Copyright J. S. Drucker. Courtesy of the artist.

p. 255 Styrofoam cup with ballpoint pen inscriptions found in downtown Brooklyn, October 1995. Photographs by Angela Cumberbirch.

PACIFIC ILLUSTRATIONS

PUBLISHERS

P|I

Pacific Illustrations is currently reviewing new works of fiction, translation, and non-fiction.

Please send manuscripts to Pacific Illustrations, Inc., 198 Broadway, room 806, New York, NY 10038.

Manuscripts cannot be returned unless accompanied by a self-addressed stamped envelope.

Back Issues of Grand Street

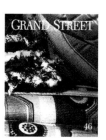
An Indispensable Collection

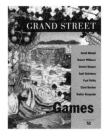
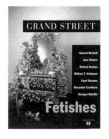

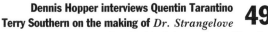
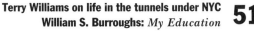

Now Available–Order While They Last

CALL 1-800-807-6548 or send name, address, issue number(s), and quantity.
American Express, Mastercard, and Visa accepted; please send credit card number
and expiration date. Back issues are $15.00 each ($18.00 overseas and Canada),
including postage and handling, payable in U.S. dollars. Address orders to *Grand Street*
Back Issues, 131 Varick Street, Suite 906, New York, NY 10013.

Some of the bookstores where

GRAND STREET

can be found :

Black Oak Books, Berkeley, CA
Bookstore Fiona, Carson, CA
University of California Books, Irvine, CA
Museum of Contemporary Art, Los Angeles, CA
Occidental College Bookstore, Los Angeles, CA
Diesel Books, Oakland, CA
City Lights, San Francisco, CA
Logos, Santa Cruz, CA
Arcana, Santa Monica, CA
Small World Books, Venice, CA
Stone Lion Books, Fort Collins, CO
Yale Co-op, New Haven, CT
University of Connecticut Bookstore, Storrs, CT
Bookworks, Washington, DC
Oxford Bookstore, Atlanta, GA
Iowa Book & Supply, Iowa City, IA
Prairie Lights, Iowa City, IA
University Books, Iowa City, IA
Seminary Co-op, Chicago, IL
Von's Book Shop, West Lafayette, IN
Carmichael's, Louisville, KY
Waterstone's Books, Boston, MA
M.I.T. Press Bookstore, Cambridge, MA
Nantucket Books, Nantucket, MA
Broadside Books, Northampton, MA
Provincetown Books, Provincetown, MA
Books Etc., Portland, ME
Book Beat, Oak Park, MI
Baxter's Books, Minneapolis, MN

Walker Art Center Books, Minneapolis, MN
Hungry Mind Bookstore, St. Paul, MN
Whistler's, Kansas City, MO
Left Bank Books, St. Louis, MO
Nebraska Bookstore, Lincoln, NE
Dartmouth Books, Hanover, NH
Micawber Books, Princeton, NJ
Salt of the Earth, Albuquerque, NM
Collected Works, Santa Fe, NM
Community Books, Brooklyn, NY
Talking Leaves, Buffalo, NY
Book Revue, Huntington, NY
The Bookery, Ithaca, NY
Doubleday Books, New York, NY
Gotham Book Mart, New York, NY
St. Mark's Bookstore, New York, NY
Wendell's Books, New York, NY
UC Bookstore, Cincinnati, OH
Books & Co., Dayton, OH
Looking Glass Books, Portland, OR
Farley's Bookshop, New Hope, PA
Bradd Alan Books, Philadelphia, PA
Joseph Fox Books, Philadelphia, PA
College Hill, Providence, RI
Chapter Two Books, Charleston, SC
Open Book, Greenville, SC
Xanadu Bookstore, Memphis, TN
DiverseBooks, Houston, TX
Sam Weller's, Salt Lake City, UT
Williams Corner, Charlottesville, VA
Studio Art Shop, Charlottesville, VA
Northshire Books, Manchester, VT
Woodland Patter, Milwaukee, WI